THE
HEALY-RAES
A Twenty-Four Seven Political Legacy

Dedicated to my wife, Kathleen,
and to our beloved grandchildren, Aidan, Caitlin, Dan and Oran.

THE
HEALY-RAES

A Twenty–Four Seven Political Legacy

DONAL HICKEY

RUSHY MOUNTAIN BOOKS

First published in 2015 by
Rushy Mountain Books,
Tiernaboul, Killarney,
Co Kerry.
Tel: 0872453891
Email: donal@rushymountainbooks.com

www.rushymountainbooks.com

ISBN: 978-0-9934633-0-3

© Donal Hickey, 2015

Printed by Tralee Printing Works. www.traleeprinting.com

Layout and design by Cathal Cudden,
Bright Idea, Fossa, Killarney. www.brightidea.ie

Cover photo: Valerie O'Sullivan. Back cover photo: Don MacMonagle.

Contents

The Author

DONAL HICKEY was the south-west correspondent for Examiner Newspapers, Cork, for 40 years, having previously worked with *The Kerryman* and *The Corkman*, and a regular current affairs commentator on the broadcast media. With a keen interest in politics, he covered every local, general and presidential election since 1973 and has reported on three generations of Healy-Raes since the 1970's.

He was also the Irish Examiner's environment correspondent, for several years, and continues to write a weekly column in the newspaper on the subject.

His previous books include the best-selling *The Mighty Healy-Rae* (1997), *Stone Mad For Music* (1999), both published by Marino, and *Beyond The Pale* (2007), published by Mentor Books.

He has also contributed to numerous publications, has edited several works and has been editor of the critically-acclaimed local history publication, *Sliabh Luachra Journal*, since its foundation in 1981. A native of Gneeveguilla, Co Kerry, he lives in Killarney.

Acknowledgements

A book like this could not be written without the support of many people. Although I knew the late Jackie Healy-Rae for all of his 38 years as an elected representative, it was also necessary to talk with many others to fill out what was a very full, hectic and often turbulent career. My first book on him, almost 20 years ago, was based on the campaign that saw him elected to the Dail for the first time and how, as an Independent TD, he came to prop up a Bertie Ahern-led government in return for projects for his Kerry South constituency.

The story has moved on considerably since then and there are now two new generations of elected Healy-Raes, creating a powerful and nationally-regarded political dynasty. I have attempted to trace the growth and expansion of the organisation to the present day.

Firstly, I wish to thank the Healy-Rae family and Kathleen Cahill for their co-operation and for photographs from family albums. Thanks also to some of their supporters, and rivals, for sharing insights and providing anecdotes on the life and times of a most interesting family.

Journalistic colleagues have been unfailingly supportive – people such as Michael O'Regan, Paschal Sheehy, Aidan O'Connor, Micheal Lehane, Anne Lucey, Owen O'Shea, Ray Ryan and Breda Joy - and especially Con Dennehy, author of the outstanding book, *Tough As Leather*, on world champion mountain runner John Lenihan. Con has been most generous with his advice.

Thanks also to professional photographers Don MacMonagle, Eamon Keogh, Michelle Cooper-Galvin, Valerie O'Sullivan and Naomi Gaffey, whose images greatly enhance the book.

I also acknowledge the excellence of graphic designer Cathal Cudden, of Bright Idea, Killarney, who ensured the book was produced to a high standard and to Tralee Printing Works for a top quality publication. Finally, thanks to my wife, Kathleen, and family for their help and patience, with the internet/social media, in particular.

Prologue

"Without doubt, after Neil Blaney, Jackie Healy-Rae was the best political operator I ever came across."
JOHN O'LEARY, KERRY FIANNA FÁIL TD FOR 31 YEARS.

Who could ever have thought a member of that much-maligned species, the Irish political class, would be compared to a saint?

A priest at Jackie Healy-Rae's funeral Mass raised a few eyebrows when he likened the politician to St John Paul 11. Fr Con Buckley may have stretched matters, but he could have called him St Jackie and nobody would have disagreed. Monday December 8, 2014, was a day for eulogies only.

The Kilgarvan padre recalled the hardship of the politician's youth in the wet and heathery land along the southern foothills of Mangerton Mountain. It was this spartan upbringing that moulded a personality that remained forever rooted and in close touch with the plain people, he surmised. "I'm reminded of John Paul 11 who broke stones in a quarry for a living in early life; Jackie also learned in the real school of ordinary life and people. And, like John Paul, they were the ones he always served," he told mourners.

Upwards of 1,000 people filled St Patrick's Church, which dominates Kilgarvan from rising ground ground at the Kenmare side of the village. Hundreds more gathered outside. Many household names were in the pews, but the congregation was made up mainly of everyday folk; the type of people that voted for Jackie Healy-Rae and continue to loyally support the political dynasty he founded.

The President and Taoiseach were represented by their uniformed aide-de-camps. Two former taoisigh were there as well as countless deputies, senators, councillors, members of the European Parliament, musicians and long-retired hurlers and footballers. Not bad for a man who once sold rails of turf for a living.

In the days following his death on Friday December 5, fulsome tributes poured in. Predictably, the most frequently used word was 'colourful'. "He fought tooth and nail for the people he loved," said former Taoiseach Bertie Ahern whose governments Jackie Healy-Rae had supported.

Fr Buckley's panegyric was in harmony with the tributes that gushed forth with the fluency of the cascading River Roughty in full spate as it tumbles towards Kenmare and the Atlantic. 'Massive' was one of the late politician's favourite adjectives and his funeral could be so described.

Thousands flocked to Kilgarvan on Saturday and Sunday, silently filing past his remains which lay in repose in the family public house in the heart of the village. Some queued for hours, whiling the time away by recounting their meetings with the politician and favours he had done for them. It was the biggest funeral Kilgarvan had ever seen, reckoned by his son, Danny, to have been attended by 10,000.

While powerful people were important and essential to Jackie Healy-Rae when it came to securing deals for the constituency, he would have taken greater satisfaction from the legions of so-called 'plain people' who came to pay their final respects. Like the man himself, the farewell was something out of the ordinary, with a deal of stage management.

Even Peg, his pet pony, entered the scene amid more than a little drama as the cortege made its way at a ceremonially slow pace through the village.

It was entirely apt that a dynamic life lived in the public eye should end in such a style. Jackie Healy-Rae loved being a public figure and the centre of attention. He moved among his people with the easy familiarity of Ruby Walsh riding winners at Cheltenham and duly accepted their acclaim. But a saint could not have survived as long as he did in a tough, unforgiving game and he was as capable as any of his opponents at pulling off political deals and strokes.

With one era over, people were looking to the future. The Healy-Rae legacy was embodied in two sons and a grandson who are ensuring the family's political profile remains high. Typically enough, Michael Healy-Rae ticked off his father's rivals when he spoke at the end of the Mass. In what amounted to a political speech, he told them they shouldn't be taking credit for things Da had done. "That's my boy," you could almost hear Da say.

Let the story roll…

My Mother was a Miracle

It all started from nothing. A veritable, rags-to-riches story of a humble rural family, out of which grew what is today, arguably, Ireland's most successful political dynasty, as well as a thriving, hands-on set of businesses built on an innate spirit of enterprise and hard work.

In 1931, the first electric shavers went on sale in America; the Star-Spangled Banner officially became the US national anthem, screen star Charlie Chaplin was awarded France's distinguished Legion of Honour, and Jackie Healy-Rae was born. Danny and Mary Healy, a hard-working, farming couple of modest means, hardly regarded the birth of their first child, on March 9, as something of significance to the wider world. But they were proud of their baby boy who was christened, John Patrick, and who would become known nationally as Jackie Healy-Rae.

Life in the 1930's was grim for many people, including this family. "I had no money. Not a penny. We'd be starved only for Mrs Quill (a local shopkeeper)!" Jackie recalled, as an old man recounting days of his youth.

At least four generations of Healys have farmed at Reacaisleach, a Gaelic name for a townland which translates as rough, grazing land. The commonly used version of the name is 'Rae' and it became part of the family name to distinguish them from other Healys in the area. The farm lies about two miles from the village of Kilgarvan, in south Kerry, up to 65 acres in all including a number of bogs, in the shadows of Mangerton Mountain. Jackie's father cut turf for the homestead, while people from the village like the Quills and the Healy-Shines would pay him £1 or £1.50 for the right

OPPOSITE: Jackie Healy-Rae with his mare, Peg.

to cut turf there every year. That helped keep the family turning over, as they would say.

The family would be among 'the plain people of Ireland who eat their dinner in the middle of the day' – Jackie's reputed definition of his core political supporters.

Jackie's great grandfather and a brother shared the same house, one in a thatched half and the other in a slated half. There wasn't enough space for both, so his great granduncle moved a short distance away to make fields out of mountainy land, digging out rocks to build ditches which are still there. That branch of the family was known as the 'Tim Dens'.

One of Jackie's earliest memories was of calling to the home of the neighbouring Lynch family. Tom Lynch and his wife used to smoke clay pipes, but they didn't always have tobacco. Jackie would break soft turf for them, which he would stuff into the pipes, then lighting the pipes with a spark from the open fire. And away they'd puff. Those were the days of the perpetually open door in rural Ireland. People drifted casually in and out of each other's houses without ever feeling the need to knock, or announce their arrival.

Jackie's father milked six cows and kept a horse for ploughing. They had a 'comharing', or co-operative system, with other families in the locality. A neighbour would come with a horse in early spring, for instance, so they would have two horses working together making ridges for the potato garden. Danny would, of course, return the favour. "If we hadn't potatoes, we wouldn't exist. There was no way," Jackie remembered. No spud ever fell to the floor in that house.

Most people were poor; very poor by today's standards. It was much worse than what has become regarded as austerity in 21st century Ireland. Housing was of Third World standard. Electricity had not yet to come to most parts of rural Ireland and there was no running water. People needed help from one another to survive. They depended on each other.

When Jackie came into the world, the fledgling Irish Free State was still struggling to find its feet. Eamon de Valera formed the first Fianna Fáil government in 1932, with the support of the Labour party. The government decided to withhold land annuities from Britain – instalments payable by farmers towards the cost of buying out the landlords. Britain retaliated by taxing imports of Irish cattle and so began the 'economic war' which lasted for over six years and which worsened the effects on Ireland of the global economic depression in the 1930s. It was a dreadful period during which the market for cattle collapsed and farmers sold their livestock for a pittance. Then followed World War Two, with rationing of food and fuel. Easy to understand, therefore, that hardship was part of life for people like the Healy-Raes. Then, on a day in early February when Jackie was eight years old, the family suffered a setback that was to have life-changing implications.

In the field behind their house, Danny was tipping up a horse-load of manure for the garden when he damaged a disc in his back. He was taken to Kenmare Hospital where a doctor decided to bathe him in extra-hot water. Danny got a bad fright and suffered severe pain. The hope was that the hot water and steam would remedy his back, but such was not to be. It only made his condition worse and Danny never did a day's work again, being disabled for the remaining 24 years of his life.

Mary was left with the responsibility of providing for their six children. Danny had been previously married, but his wife died leaving him with six children. He later married Mary (Riordan), who hailed from Coomlougha, not too far away. The Riordans were known as exceptionally strong people and willing workers.

One of the sons from Danny's first marriage, Timmy, was of exceptional help to Mary and she took over the running of the farm, as well as raising her young family. She also found time to bake delightful bread and make butter at home. Any surplus butter would be sent to Quill's shop, in Kilgarvan village.

As Mary had no social welfare, every penny had to be earned. Much of what would be seen as a man's work had to be done by her. Being the eldest, Jackie had to help his mother and often told in later life how they survived by cutting turf, selling ricks of turf and horse-rails of turf in the village for £1. While still very young, he acquired basic skills like cutting skillauns (seed potatoes), wielding a slean and setting a range of vegetables.

Jackie fondly remembered Danny's two families being very close and he worshipped Timmy. One by one, most of the first family emigrated,

Jackie Healy-Rae, 1947.

mainly to England, but they remained in contact with Rae, which they also continued to visit throughout their lives. The 'step' in the family didn't matter much: they were really all one, age gaps notwithstanding. Timmy was the last to go, ending up in Birmingham. Jackie also made a wheelchair for his father with two bicycle wheels and a pram wheel, an axle and the seat of chair, with rests for his elbows.

According to Jackie, they would not have survived without the help of the shopkeeper Quill family, of whom they were customers. He never forgot a time in 1947 when his mother had no money to buy flour. Mrs Quill, however, sent up a 10-stone sack which was left on the ditch at Rae crossroads. His mother went to collect it. She slung it on her back and brought it across the bog and fields. Exhausted, she landed the heavy sack on a seat in the kitchen. Not a single grain of that flour was wasted.

Mary lived to be 96. Interviewed by Tralee historian Maurice O'Keeffe for the Irish Life and Lore series not long before his death, Jackie described his mother as 'a fierce woman altogether, extraordinary and a miracle'.

Much of the responsibility for supporting the family fell on Jackie's young shoulders. The sale of calves and turf kept them ticking over. Money garnered from the sale of their six calves every year was essential to keep body and soul together. They once lost their most valuable calf, a devastating event that was seared into Jackie's memory. It was a strawberry heifer, red and white with spots. One day when he went down the fields to check on the animals he saw the 'strawberry' lying on its back, its four legs pointing to the sky. It had died during the night. Jackie raced home in tears to his mother, wondering how he would break the bad news to her. They were devastated: their bread and butter had been taken for a time.

He once said that he never walked to school: he ran because there was always work to be done before and after school. Seven o'clock never found him in bed in the morning. When there was pressing work to be done on the farm in the spring and summer, he would ask the teacher to be allowed home early. He left school at 13 and never sat an exam. Throughout his life, people sometimes noted that he trotted rather than walked. Part of his childhood that never left him.

In the late 1940s, Jackie, now well into his teens, needed a job off-farm. Work was very scarce but Tom Randles, of Kilgarvan, hired him to drive a hackney car, or rural taxi. The car was a Ford Prefect and his pay was £1 per week. In those days, few people owned cars so hackney drivers were kept busy. One day, Jackie drove some people to the County Home (now St Columbanus) in Killarney, where a man from Kilgarvan had died. As there was no hearse available, a question arose: how would they get the remains back to Kilgarvan?

Ever the practical man, Jackie figured there was only one thing to do – put the coffin on the roof of the Prefect, a fairly small car. The deceased was a light little man, but the weight of the coffin itself was a worry. They struck off for Kilgarvan and, as the car nosed around the corner of the village, they could see a funeral crowd had gathered. Tom Randles came out of his house with a cup tea in his hand. He was curious to find out who was bringing the coffin. Tom feared the cloth roof of his car would collapse and the cup fell from his hand with the shock of it. "My fecking car is ruined forever," he declared.

Not long after that bizarre experience, Jackie went to work in forestry locally with Robert Lyne. Both men had ramshackle bikes and one of the first things they did was to buy two new bikes on hire purchase at a rate of £1 per month for 36 months. They laboured hard with spades, pickaxes and shovels and Jackie trebled his pay from the days he had worked driving for Tom Randles. Lyne eventually left to take up a post the Automobile Association (AA), in Ennis, Co Clare, and later built up a chain of hotels in Clare and Kerry.

In 1953 at the age of 22, Jackie went to America on a six-month visa with his wife-to-be Julie. She was born in America and was also a Healy. They married in St Patrick's Cathedral, New York, on August 6 that year. He worked in a cold store and his boss was an Irish-American man, 'one of the biggest blackguards I met since I came into this world'.

The huge cold store, he recalled, was as big as a field and if the boss

6

took a dislike to an employee he would give orders that involved spending a lot of time in the chilling temperatures, cold enough to freeze a drop in a man's nose. The boss had a sadistic streak and would direct a worker to go looking for something that wasn't even in the cold store, leaving an unfortunate there for a long time.

In America at that time, jobs were scarce so Jackie had to put up with it. But he never liked the place; he and Julie returned to Ireland in December 1953 and he was soon back farming in Rae.

Sampling very little of New York nightlife, he saved his dollars. It was a

The family at Rae, 1950's. From left: Mick, Kathy, Jackie, Hannie (with Jackie's baby son, Danny), Daniel, Mary, Denny and Dan.

depressed era back home and, consequently, exceptionally high emigration to America. Jackie harboured thoughts of returning to New York where a job was waiting for him. But he had always strived to make a go of things at home and, through all the gloom of a particularly dark decade in Ireland, saw possibilities of making a living in Kilgarvan.

One of his first moves was to purchase a hackney car, a Chevrolet for £460, in 1954. He also bought a small, second-hand tractor and went to work ploughing fields, making potato ridges and mowing hay for farmers. The mighty dollar was talking! He was helped by his brother, Denny, and they took on all the work that was going, operating round the clock when necessary. He could see that farming ways were changing; agriculture was slowly becoming more mechanised and the horse was beginning to give way to the tractor.

And he also enjoyed his jaunts as a hackney driver. One of his memorable trips was to the 1955 All-Ireland football final between Kerry and Dublin. Patsy Quill, a returned yank, and his wife hired his car and asked him to take a circuitous route to Croke Park via Waterford and Wicklow.

The so-called 'Dublin machine' had been raging hot favourites to win the All-Ireland. Driving into Bray on the eve of the match, Jackie stopped to buy an evening newspaper. Turning to the back page, he read a headline to the effect that one of Dublin's top players, Kevin Heffernan, would teach Ned Roche, of Kerry, a football lesson. "I thought to myself we might as well turn around and go away home again, but sure Kerry beat 'em well," he recalled for Maurice O'Keeffe.

For a man who grew up in an area where traditional music and dance were among the principal means of entertainment, much of it home-based, it might come as a surprise to some that Jackie's favourite instrument was the saxophone. Jazz was his preferred music. Like many other young musicians in the area, he was a self-taught melodeon player, reaching a level of proficiency that enabled him to play at house dances and, later, in dancehalls. He was a member of three different dance bands.

There were times when he dreamed about being a full-time, professional musician and making a career out of his love of music. "The only big regret, if I have any, is that I didn't go deeper into music," he confided at a time when he was preoccupied with politics many years ago. "I really loved it and if I was a free man and back in those days again, I'd really go very deep into jazz. The jazz instruments are beautiful. Anywhere they're being played, I'm not happy till I'm there."

He played more music with his close friend and next door neighbour, Dermot Hickey, than anybody else. When Dermot, a teacher, died in the early 1990's, it knocked the heart of out Jackie as far as playing music went. Along with Dermot and others, he had played in the Kilgarvan Dance Band during the 1950's, '60's and '70's.

It was an era when there were small dancehalls, some grandiosely called 'ballrooms', in every village and at many crossroads around Ireland. Most young people didn't have cars or other mechanised transport, so they were more or less confined to their own areas and usually went to halls that were within cycling distance. As women didn't patronise pubs for much of that era, the halls were the only places for young men and women to meet in a social setting. Such meetings often led to courtship and, eventually, marriage.

Jackie, the musician.

Hence, the appellation 'ballrooms of romance'.

"When Hickey was alive, all I had to do was give one blow of the saxophone inside my own place and Hickey'd be out the back immediately with his accordion on his knee. He was a massive piano accordion player. We played all that Mick Delahunty stuff, 'American Patrol', 'Alexander's Ragtime Band', all that stuff. We played very well together, too. Since I lost Hickey, I haven't had the heart to play much, but I still take it out the odd time," he told *Hot Press* magazine in 1995.

Mick Delahunty (Mick Del) and his big band, from Clonmel, Co Tipperary, were a popular outfit on the ballroom scene for about 40 years and preceded the showband era which was ushered in the late 1950's. By 1970, the nights of the orchestra in halls and ballrooms were virtually over. While the new-fangled showbands pranced and leaped around the stage, the Delahunty and the Maurice Mulcahy big bands were the only two outfits still playing sitting down.

The Maurice Mulcahy Orchestra was based in Mitchelstown, Co Cork, and had a long-time summer residency in the Central Hotel ballroom, Ballybunion, from 1957 until 1970. Jackie was a fan of both bands, but Mick Del was his undoubted favourite. He thought Mick was a fantastic saxophone player, one of the best in Ireland. They were good friends and he was sorry to see him go.

He also took pride in playing with members of the internationally-renowned Halle Orchestra and knew Bernard O'Reilly, an Irishman in the orchestra. Some of the Halle musicians would come to Kenmare on holidays every year and he played saxophone with them at night in Lansdowne Arms Hotel. "We had some massive sessions. We'd be exchanging saxophones and tunes. They were terrific saxophonists. Mighty!" As regards current musicians, he particularly liked trumpeter Johnny Carroll, with whom he made a CD.

In 1963, Dermot Hickey built a ballroom in Kilgarvan, which has for many years been a furniture store. Dermot's hall and the Carnegie, in Kenmare, six miles away, and now a grocery store, would be packed for dances a couple of nights each week in the good old days.

All the while, Jackie maintained his love of Irish music which began to enjoy a resurgence in popularity in the 1960's, during which the Clancy Brothers and their rendering of Irish ballads were all the go in America. Comhaltas Ceoltoiri Eireann (CCE), the national organisation which promotes traditional music, song and dance, also started to spread its wings countrywide in the 1960's and Jackie was chairman of Kerry CCE for seven years, starting in the mid-1960's. Kilgarvan was the venue for both county and Munster fleadhanna cheoil and Jackie and Dermot also went to 'fleadhs' in many other parts of the country, sometimes acting as adjudicators.

Whatever about music, life on the road as a hackney driver and the fun that went with it, Jackie's main attachment was to land and machinery. Self-taught, he did most of his own repair work and maintenance and also mastered the skill of welding.

Soon, he took a critical step by buying a second tractor and never looked back from there. He started work in land reclamation and site clearance and on the roads with Kerry County Council. The business continued its upward spiral and he bought his first JCB in 1965. The contracting connection between the Healy-Rae family and the council continues, sometimes controversially, to the present day.

By the late 1960s, he had a well-established plant hire firm and was on the lookout for new business ventures. Then came an unexpected opportunity. The Railway Hotel, in the centre of Kilgarvan, had been closed when the Kerry county fleadh cheoil was staged in the village in the 1969. Jackie did everything in his power to get it reopened, but failed. So, confident the business had a future, he decided to purchase the property that December. He soon had the doors wide open and proceeded to do a 'roaring trade' in a bar many times smaller than the current operation, run by his son Danny and Danny's wife, Eileen.

It was the era of the ballad boom and a revival in the popularity of Irish music. Women, previously shy about being seen in pubs, started to enter what had traditionally been seen as a male domain. Ostensibly, they went in to dance or listen to the music but, in this new, liberal period

Jackie working with his tractor, circa 1960.

of the so-called Swinging Sixties, also started drinking alcohol. In the summer of 1970, Jackie opened a singing lounge. Soon, young, mini-skirted women, in the fashion of the era, were gracing the premises, distracting the menfolk of the area from their pints. To this day, the name JACKIE HEALY-RAE can be seen in large lettering over the door. He and Julie separated, in the 1970's, and they had a family of six: Danny, John, Joan, Denis, Rosemary and Michael.

A strong work ethic dominated his life from the beginning. Though he finished his days a successful and prosperous man - having built up pub, farming and plant hire businesses as well as a successful political career - he had little money until he was well into adulthood. "I never had any money (in younger days) and if any man ever knew the value of a pound… I'll tell you…"

Even in his old age, he would become emotional when talking about his mother whom he described as a 'master topper' and something of a financial magician, like many other women of her generation. Mary knew how to get by on scant means, metaphorically scraping the bottom of the pot.

She spent her final years in a small council house in Kilgarvan village. Her unmarried son, Dan, lived with her and they got on famously. Dan missed her greatly after she died and his own health failed, too. He died suddenly in hospital of a clot. To the end of his days, Jackie, a firm believer in the after-life, was convinced that Mary took Dan. "My mother was a miracle," he would say.

Hurling Days

Some people who were around in the mid-20th century like to think that the red and white jersey of the Kilgarvan hurling club commanded the kind respect reserved for the New Zealand rugby Haka, a traditional war dance of the Maori people. The eloquence with which the colours are explained in the club's website is redolent of the vibrant spirit of the area.

The explanation reads: "Red is a colour that represents ideals that are crucial to sport, such as confidence, adrenalin, heroism, passion and rage. The colour red has become synonymous with sporting organisations as diverse as the Cleveland Indians, Manchester United and Ferrari. Research indicates that exposure to large quantities of red prompts the release of adrenaline into the bloodstream, quickens the heart rate and engenders a sense of excitement. Those who changed from green and gold to red and white knew what they were doing."

Were Jackie, an ex-hurler, still alive he might suggest – without a hint of vainglory, of course - ah yes, that's what I'm all about, too!

Jackie Healy-Rae (ringed) with a Kilgarvan hurling team, mid-1950's

On the hurling field, he was known for speed and determination more than skill. One day he went into Denis P O'Sullivan's shop, in Kilgarvan, for a hurley and, as he came back out, was met by a local publican, Denny O'Sullivan (Roger), grandfather of current Dublin footballer and All-Ireland medal winner Cian O'Sullivan.

"Where are you going?," asked Denny. "Hurling," replied Jackie. Feigning surprise, Denny called him aside for a minute. Jackie, slightly impatient, was in a hurry and asked what he wanted.

"You're not going hurling; you're going trying to hurl," Denny elaborated. Jackie was not pleased. "I ate him," he joked many years later.

Up to his final days, Jackie would show off some of his broken bones and hurling injuries as badges of honour. He truly loved the game, putting his heart and soul into it. "I could lose the ball three times and get it back again. I had massive speed."

He and his friend, Dermot Hickey, sometimes worked their own tactics on the pitch. Jackie played at wing-forward and one day, for instance, he scooped the sliotar over a defender's head for Dermot to grab it and 'drive it out through the net'.

According to Jackie, the aforementioned Denis P was the lynchpin of Kilgarvan's hurling success, being secretary of the club and chief organiser of the game locally in the 1950s, the breakthrough decade. The dominating Kerry hurling belt, however, still comprises a cluster of six or seven rural clubs in the northern side of the county. Places like Ballyduff, Kilmoyley and Crotta have a long history with the camán. In south Kerry, Gaelic football was and is the main game, so Kilgarvan was an exception.

When Jackie Healy-Rae was growing up in the 1930s and '40s the simple things of life took pride of place in Kilgarvan. Every house did not have a radio; television was, as yet, unheard of, and newspapers were the chief sources of information. On big match days, large groups of people would gather in a house which had a radio to listen to commentator Micheál O'Hehir's broadcasts from Croke Park.

Hurling, football and athletics were the main sporting past-times in Kilgarvan and Jackie took part in all three, while also dabbling in bike racing. There was huge interest in and support for hurling, so the club was the heartbeat of the parish. The Fr Cahill Cup, presented by the local parish priest, was the premier competition for schools hurling. Youngsters played with fire and gusto for the cup, which helped Jackie develop his hurling. Although he had an arduous workload at home, his mother never begrudged him time spent on playing fields. Indeed, she was happy that he was involved, even if she pretended otherwise to some people.

In 1947, the omens were favourable for Kilgarvan's hurling fortunes. The seniors gave a reasonably good account of themselves in going under to Kilmoyley in the second round of that year's county championship, while the minors had a big win over neighbours Kenmare in the curtain-raiser. The astute Kilmoyley veteran, Mickey McGrath, was there that day and made a brave forecast that a senior championship would come to Kilgarvan in the years ahead if the under-age side could be kept together.

His prediction came to pass in 1953 when Kilgarvan won its first Kerry senior hurling title, defeating Lixnaw, 4-4 to 2-3. It was the first of three county titles in what was to be the club's most successful decade. Ten players and four substitutes in the 20-strong panel were products of the Fr Cahill Cup.

En route to the final, Kilgarvan accounted for teams like Kenmare and Crotta O'Neills, for long the lords of Kerry hurling. Years later, Denis P recalled that one of Kilgarvan's 'loudest, cheering supporters' on the day of the final was Jackie Healy-Rae, who had played in the first round. He was to leave for New York the following week. Aged 22, he was following a path across the Atlantic taken by hundreds of thousands of young Irish people in a black decade for emigration. His stay stateside was not too long, nevertheless, for he was back home again, and hurling, in 1954. Several of his siblings later went to America.

He made the senior team in '54 and '55 and really came of age when Kilgarvan won its second senior county championship in 1956. "The right wing of our attack was Thomas Randles wearing number 10 and inside him was Jackie wearing number 13, two dashing players endowed with speed, stamina, fire, spirit and scoring potential," Denis P recorded. "Jackie filled the same position in our 1958 win and again in 1959 when were beaten in the county final and he continued to function well into the 1960s."

A family group and friends at the Gleneagle Hotel, Killarney, on the occasion of the 50th wedding anniversary of Julie Healy-Rae's parents, Daniel Stephen and Hannah Healy.

Front row (from left): **Lil Purcell, Helen Murphy, Danny Healy-Rae, Jackie (with daughter Rosemary), Denis Healy-Rae, Daniel Stephen Healy, Hannah Healy, Julie, Joan Healy-Rae, John Healy-Rae, Maureen Hickey.**

Second row: **Bob Purcell, Jackie Brosnan, John O'Leary TD, Judy O'Leary, Eileen Galvin, Nora Healy-Rae, Kathleen Brosnan, Audrey O'Sullivan, Molly Healy, Thomas Doyle, Dermot Hickey, Florrie O'Sullivan.**

Back: **Jerh Quill, Mrs Quill, John Galvin, Nora Doyle, Mary O'Sullivan, Timmy Buckley, Tim Healy, Michael O'Sullivan.**

But the golden era of Kilgarvan hurling had passed. "Yes," Denis P noted ruefully, "the red and white of Kilgarvan was feared and respected but, unlike the babbling brook, our gallant band could not go on forever."

For all his days playing hurling, one of Jackie's longest memories arose from a football match between Kilgarvan and Kenmare, as illustrated by a story he told to well-known sports journalist and former Kerry hurler John Barry, in *The Kerryman* newspaper, in June 1970.

"It was the final of the Murphy Cup and we were trying to win it for the first time. We were leading up to about three minutes from the end, but then Tony Murphy got a goal for Kenmare. We all thought that was the end for us, but about a minute from the end I got a ball out in the corner from Sean Healy. I made tracks towards the goal and succeeded in getting inside the Kenmare full-back.

"There was the goalkeeper facing me – James Brosnan, the chemist in Kenmare – and I was such a bad footballer I hardly knew what to do. Anyway, I threw the ball down to kick it and James Brosnan dived on my boot to smother the shot. But, do you know what happened? The ball hit my knee on the way down and went forward into the Kenmare net.

"I scored the winning goal and if it wasn't the greatest fluke of all time I don't know what it was! That was some night in Kilgarvan. I was brought home on the top of Denzie Hegarty's car with the cup and we celebrated in rare style. Guess I was born lucky."

And, yes, some lucky breaks were also to mark his political career. Like sport, the road of life itself can have strange and unexpected turns. To his own amazement, he was to have access to some of most powerful people in Ireland in the decades ahead.

— 2 —

Getting Involved in Politics

In his own words, Jackie Healy-Rae was 'Fianna Fáil born and suckled', but was in his mid-thirties before he became active in the party. It was a 1966 by-election in his Kerry South constituency that got him going as a foot soldier.

The by-election resulted from the death of Killarney-based Fianna Fáil TD Honor Mary Crowley. John O'Leary, also from Killarney, was nominated as the party candidate. It was to be a barn-storming campaign, with Fianna Fáil cabinet ministers, led by the redoubtable Neil Blaney, from Donegal, and other big hitters moving into the constituency. O'Leary was duly elected and served as a TD for 31 years.

From the start, Healy-Rae was overawed by Blaney and remained so for the remainder of his life. "There was no more famous man ever in this country - nor ever again will there be anybody fit to lace his boots - than Blaney. He was an excellent, brilliant operator altogether," he said much later.

The feeling was somewhat mutual: Blaney was also impressed by this energetic and fearless Fianna Fáil trooper. He soon spotted Healy-Rae's flair for organisation and razzmatazz and recruited him to his team for other by-elections around the country, to which he would bring fire, literally, and huge splashes of colour.

By the late 1960's, Healy-Rae was one of the most flamboyant characters in Fianna Fáil, ever before he stood for election. In his book, *On The Doorsteps – memoirs of a long-serving TD*, John O'Leary observed Healy-Rae could talk about anything; was a great man to tell a story and give a humorous twist to any yarn; outgoing and entertaining. "Despite being so colourful and witty, he could be very serious too, especially when it came to elections. He was a great man to give political advice and always had his feet firmly planted on the ground. He had a brilliant reputation as an organiser…his style of public speaking was much the same as Blaney's; he could get the people going and get them laughing and clapping. Healy-Rae certainly stood out from the crowd."

In 1973, Healy-Rae got his big break, politically, when a Fianna Fáil seat became vacant on Kerry County Council following the unexpected death of a veteran councillor for the Killarney area, Michael Doherty. Some people in the party urged him to put his name before a convention, something he had in mind for some time anyway.

Then, one day, a tall, elderly man wearing a hat, whom he did not know, walked into his bar in Kilgarvan. After the man began to converse, Jackie asked him who he was. He was Batty (The Smith) Cronin, from Tureencahill, close to the Cork/Kerry border. Batty and his family had been involved with the IRA during 'the troubles'; he was a high priest in Fianna Fáil and an admirer of Eamon de Valera. Batty asked a few questions of Jackie – what was he doing and what were his ambitions? Jackie calculated, rightly, that Batty had come to size him up and then report back to the Fianna Fáil elders.

Some weeks later, one of the first people Jackie saw arriving at the convention was Batty, a gentle giant of a blacksmith with the biggest pair of hands ever seen on a man, they used to say. Jackie was nominated for co-option and he heard later that Batty had given a positive report about him – that he was a livewire who would work hard as a councillor and benefit the party.

Healy-Rae narrowly won through at the convention, defeating Jim Doherty, a nephew of the late Cllr Doherty, by just one vote. He was duly co-opted to the seat and started working day and night to raise his profile in preparation for the 1974 local elections. Recalling the co-option, John O'Leary said he had Healy-Rae in the mind for the seat so that he could keep an eye on a man who was becoming more active in the party locally and who, obviously, had ambitions. "Even though I didn't see him as a threat to my Dáil seat, I knew he would probably be interested in a career beyond the council in the fullness of time."

It didn't take Healy-Rae long to make his mark on the council. Very soon, he was being reported in *The Kerryman* for his sometimes outlandish statements at meetings. One day, when complaining about a rat-infested public dump, outside Killarney, he claimed the rodents were so numerous there they were saluting him as he drove to council meetings. The county engineer played down the claim, saying he had no such experience. A headline in that week's paper read: "Rats recognise councillor but not county engineer".

A short time after entering the council, a matter which his son, Danny, and grandson, Johnny, are still trying to resolve was brought to his attention. Farmers on the Kilgarvan side of Mangerton Mountain received a letter from the Killarney National Park authorities telling them to keep their sheep out of the park.

Pictured in Kilgarvan during an election campaign in the early 1980's were, from left: Jackie's mother, Mary; Fianna Fáil leader Charlie Haughey, Dan Healy-Rae, Jackie Healy-Rae.

The farmers sought a meeting with Jackie. After a long discussion, he turned the story around the other way and urged the farmers to write back to the national park bosses asking them to prevent deer from the park from trespassing on farmers' land. A letter was duly sent back and no more was heard about the matter. Deer trespass continues to be an important issue, more than 40 years on.

Deputy O'Leary was making note of what Healy-Rae was up to and, when the 1974 local elections came round, decided to run himself. This was partly because Healy-Rae was beginning to take credit for some things in the Killarney area that he was responsible for, O'Leary later claimed. Like any TD, O'Leary had to watch his back from possible upstarts in his own party and figured he could mark Healy-Rae a bit closer by being on the council himself.

A convention chose Healy-Rae, O'Leary and Tom Fleming (father of the current Kerry Independent TD, also Tom Fleming) as the Fianna Fáil candidates. According to O'Leary, Healy-Rae was raging after the convention, claiming O'Leary was out to take his council seat. O'Leary tried to calm him down and it was to be the start of a sometimes fraught relationship between the two men, which was to last until O'Leary retired as a TD, in 1997.

All three Fianna Fáil candidates were elected to the council for the Killarney area in 1974, with Healy-Rae topping the poll. O'Leary maintained afterwards he had been generous to Healy-Rae in the division of the area for vote management purposes.

Later in 1974, this writer was a witness to Healy-Rae's electioneering skills. By this time, he had built up a reputation in Fianna Fáil as an organiser of torch-lit, final rallies at by-elections around the country. "We arranged bonfires, we arranged torches, we arranged goalpost crossbars that lit up with sods of turf," he explained. "They were spectacular. One man would stand at one side of the goalpost and another fella at the other side, both holding up big turf torches. The crossbar was lined up with cans and a burning sod of turf in each can. The sods would be soaked in petrol and diesel oil so that they'd burn brightly. There'd be two or three bands out in front playing. It was a beautiful sight to see as you were coming into a town. We'd get massive crowds along to the rallies in the last two or three days before the votes were cast."

I happened to be in Mallow, Co Cork, on an evening during the 1974 by-election in Cork North East and can testify to the veracity of the above account. As a young reporter covering the by-election for *The Corkman* newspaper, I was standing on the side of the street with colleague Ray Ryan, of the *The Cork Examiner*.

All of a sudden, a gleaming white Mercedes pulled up at the West End. The driver, who was wearing an astrakhan hat, and his passenger jumped out, opened the boot and started throwing out sods of turf. Healy-Rae was the man in the distinctive headgear. His passenger was none other than Maurice Galvin, a psychiatric nurse from Killarney and a close friend who regularly accompanied Healy-Rae on such expeditions.

They had been part of Blaney's by-election team for several years and had built up expertise in creating election fireworks. Sometimes, Donie (Mackey) O'Shea, of Killarney, provided transport and tyres for bonfires.

Soon, two lines of men formed up in the centre of Mallow. They started walking towards O'Brien Street, each man holding aloft a pike topped with a blazing sod. Healy-Rae ran along the top of the street near the courthouse, spilling petrol out of a gallon. Another man then threw a match on the street and a flame took off down the hill. It looked for a moment as if the street was on fire, a spectacle that fuelled the palpable excitement of the evening. Throughout his life, Healy-Rae believed traditional tactics to secure voters' attention were best, with torch-lit, final rallies being an essential part of the last push for votes in the dying days of a campaign.

After the flames had died, many Fianna Fáil luminaries went to the Central Hotel, in Mallow, where, again, Healy-Rae was the centre of attention. In the presence of the late John Wilson and other leading figures in the party, he provided further entertainment by whistling and step-dancing at the same time in the hotel lounge.

The 1974 by-election was caused by the death of Fianna Fáil TD Liam

Ahern and the Fianna Fáil candidate, Sean Brosnan, a Youghal-based barrister, was elected. Brosnan was a native of Dingle and a winner of three All-Ireland football medals with Kerry.

A Fine Gael/Labour coalition was in office from 1973 to '77. In the early months of 1977, it became clear an election was not far away. It was a troubled period and the Liam Cosgrave-led Government had difficulty in grappling with record levels of inflation, unemployment and national debt. The country was in a state of economic recession and the Government was unpopular. One minister even became known on Frank Hall's satirical programme on RTE television as the Minister for Hardship.

In the sporting lexicon, Fianna Fáil would be playing with a strong wind whenever the ball was thrown in. The party, unaccustomed to opposition, was put on an election footing. As Jackie Healy-Rae would say decades later, fellows started 'to buy oil for the chains of their bikes'.

Early into the campaign in Kerry South, however, a row flared inside Fianna Fáil and it centred on Healy-Rae's pivotal role as director of elections. His loyalty to the party was being questioned in the light of his continuing support for Neil Blaney, long after the former Cabinet minister and elections supremo from Donegal had been kicked out of Fianna Fáil in the wake of the 1970 Arms Crisis.

Healy-Rae made no secret of his support for Blaney, also making strident calls at Ard Fheiscanna for his return to the party. There was even speculation in the mid-seventies that Healy-Rae might run as an independent, Blaney-type candidate. All of which caused some unease to John O'Leary as a sitting Fianna Fáil TD in Kerry South. O'Leary made his concerns known to senior figures in the party in Dublin. According to O'Leary, the party bosses suggested that Healy-Rae, who by now was building up a formidable, personal support base in Fianna Fáil, be challenged directly to state his unequivocal loyalty to the party. "I had decided his wings needed to be clipped a bit," revealed O'Leary in his memoir.

Healy-Rae had already been appointed director of elections for O'Leary and the other Fianna Fáil TD in the constituency Timothy (Chub) O'Connor, but the Comhairle Dáil Ceanntair, the Fianna Fáil ruling body for the constituency, decided to call a meeting, in March 1977, with just one item on the agenda - to reconsider the position of director of elections.

There were leaks to the local media in advance of the meeting which took place in a High Noon-type atmosphere in the Grand Hotel, Killarney, the unofficial Fianna Fáil headquarters locally at the time. It is remembered in Killarney as the night men came down from the hills. Some of their weather-beaten faces sported long, bushy side whiskers. An assortment of male headgear was on display, but peaked caps and round hats dominated. Healy-Rae supporters were in town.

The gloves were off. There were clear divisions between the O'Leary and Healy-Rae camps and their backers who assembled that night. O'Leary told the meeting he had been approached by some people in the party who were concerned about the director of elections and the air needed to be cleared. The party had to be sure of the absolute loyalty of every member going into an election, he stated.

Some of the speeches were fiery; others measured. Healy-Rae declared his loyalty and full commitment to running a 'mighty campaign' for the party, which he had no intention of leaving. Nor would he be a candidate himself for Blaney, or anyone else. That satisfied the meeting. Any doubts O'Leary had about Healy-Rae's support base in Fianna Fáil were dispelled that tension-filled night. A large number of 'Rae' supporters cheered loudly after the meeting and triumphantly shouldered their man out onto the street as if he were an All-Ireland winning Kerry football captain. They celebrated his endorsement as director of elections and as a loyal Fianna Fáil man.

O'Leary, however, knew that if there was a slight swing against Chub, or himself, or if either of them lost their seat, there was now a man ready and waiting to jump in. "I also knew that he (Healy-Rae) was one of the best electioneers in the country and I wanted him inside the tent for the campaign. He seemed to be genuine in what he'd said at the meeting and I was glad I had brought the issue to a head."

Some of the party elders, such as leading Killarney businessman Michael (Mackey) O'Shea, JB Healy and Liam Cousins, called for calm at the meeting.

They didn't want to lose an organiser of Healy-Rae's dynamism and ability. Wise counsel won on the night; the party closed ranks and left Healy-Rae in his job. "The outcome of the meeting, which was widely expected to result in the removal of Mr Healy-Rae from the sensitive post of director," reported Tony Meade in *The Kerryman*, "was very much a surprise, not only for those who expected a defeat for Healy-Rae, but also for those who were his partisans."

O'Leary would probably have been better off not to have looked for the meeting, which only served to copperfasten Healy-Rae's position and profile in Fianna Fáil. It was a show of force by Healy-Rae who then got down to the serious business of winning an election. Drawing on his encyclopaedic knowledge of Kerry South and of where the party's votes were, he divided the constituency as evenly as he could between the two candidates.

The idea was to ensure the most effective vote management, which Healy-Rae often achieved, so that both candidates would be returned. When he felt it necessary, he would reprimand a candidate and order him to stay out of the other candidate's designated area. For example, he directed O'Leary to stay away from Milltown, which had been staked as Chub's turf. So, O'Leary stayed out when the Fianna Fáil leader Jack Lynch stopped in the village during a constituency tour.

"But, it was a strategy that worked," recalled O'Leary. "We had vote management down to a tee and when the votes were counted, Chub and I ended up with about 24 per cent of the vote each and we swept back into the Dáil in the (Jack) Lynch-led landslide. I was particularly pleased to top the poll in Kerry South."

O'Leary had a first preference vote of 8,002, with Chub in second place on 7,917. Healy-Rae was praised for an outstanding campaign and for bringing in the two candidates together, with little or no vote wastage from Fianna Fáil's point or view. Fine Gael's Michael Begley took the third seat, with 6,655 first preferences. The Liam Cosgrave-led administration suffered a heavy defeat and Fianna Fáil, under Jack Lynch, who was at the summit of his popularity, gained a 20-seat majority after campaigning on giveaway policies, including the abolition of car tax and domestic rates.

Fianna Fáil took four of the six seats in Kerry. Senator Kit Ahern, from

Jackie Healy-Rae celebrates with John O'Leary and John O'Donoghue after O'Donoghue was elected a Fianna Fáil TD for the first time in 1987. (© macmonagle.com)

Ballybunion, was elected for the first time as a Fianna Fáil TD in Kerry North alongside Tom McEllistrim, a member of one of Kerry's political dynasties. Labour's Dan Spring was also elected in Kerry North. Writing in *The Kerryman*, Tony Meade said it was a magnificent double for Fianna Fáil. "In Kerry South, Jackie Healy-Rae preened himself as his two candidates coasted home more or less neck and neck."

Fianna Fáil's performance in Kerry, in 1977, was in striking contrast to what happened in 2011 general election when the party failed to win a single a seat in the county. And, ironically, the Healy-Raes played a role in keeping Fianna Fáil out, in 2011.

The next general election was in 1981 and Jackie Healy-Rae, sensing that Chub O'Connor could be edged out, was among the candidates seeking a Fianna Fáil nomination in Kerry South. After 1977, O'Connor had given indications it would be his last election. However, Healy-Rae failed to come through a convention which had a directive to select two candidates, who turned out to be outgoing deputies O'Leary and O'Connor.

A young John O'Donoghue, Caherciveen, was controversially added to the 1981 ticket. O'Donoghue's entry to the contest caused havoc with vote management plans and O'Connor, by now well into seventies, lost his seat. O'Leary was elected with Labour's Michael Moynihan and Fine Gael's Michael Begley.

As a councillor, Healy-Rae derided one body more than any other. An Taisce, the national trust for Ireland, was his nemesis. He saw An Taisce as a nuisance and an obstacle to people wishing to build houses in rural areas and could not understand objections which it lodged. In 1981, he angrily told An Taisce to keep its nose out of council business. The issue arose from a proposal by the council to redesignate as secondary special amenity seven acres owned by Ballybunion Golf Club. The land had a higher zoning of prime amenity area.

Resenting 'interference' from An Taisce, he said he did not know what the body's function was and he would break it up if he had the power. The council's planning department and councillors were quite capable of doing their job without An Taisce getting involved, he argued.

As An Taisce pointed out on many occasions, he was ignoring the body's statutory role in planning - it was entitled to be informed about planning matters and applications. "I don't give a damn about the law of the land. We're quite open to criticise the law if we think it's unreasonable. What the hell does An Taisce know about an application where a man wants to build a house for himself on his own land and why should they interfere?"

Again, An Taisce replied by saying it would not be intimidated, that Healy-Rae was wrong and that he no authority to stop An Taisce.

All his life, Healy-Rae cut turf in Rae and was an avid promoter of the traditional fuel. He tried to get the planting of trees in virgin bogland stopped and called for the development of bog roads to enable people provide their own energy rather than having to rely on expensive, imported oil. However, tree-planting went on, people continued to use oil and bog roads were left deteriorate.

While most of his proposals were practical, he would occasionally come up with ideas which were simply unworkable and didn't get support. For instance, he wanted institutions such as the new general hospital, in Tralee, opened in 1984, converted to turf-burning heating systems. When a learned engineer explained at a meeting this would be neither possible, nor practical, Healy-Rae told him: "What can you tell me about bog – a man born in the middle of it?"

In a sketch in *The Kerryman*, in June 1980, reporter Gerard Colleran wrote that Kerry County Council was only a few steps from a talking shop, but credited the Kilgarvan councillor for shooting rays of levity into a chamber which had seen its share of bad temper, listing him among the 'characters' on the council.

"In the sideshow to the real event, the lead role is played by Jackie Healy-Rae," noted Colleran, later to become editor of *The Star* newspaper and a TV3 current affairs presenter. "He's a character of much appeal and provides copy-hungry journalists with plenty of material. He talks of giant potholes in south Kerry and council trucks roaming the county at odd hours. And it's impossible to know if he really believes what he's saying. The Cossack-capped councillor from the Killarney Electoral Area provides an abiding impression of this council's first year."

Whenever a bit of fun and devilment was called for, Healy-Rae was never far away. The county council held its December 1980 meeting in Caherciveen. Having done their formal business, councillors and officials

Kerry football legend Mick O'Connell, also a former Independent member of Kerry County Council. (© macmonagle.com)

repaired to the local Ringside Rest Hotel for some Christmas celebrations. Soon, Jackie produced a 'gadget' from his car - his name for an accordion on which he belted out a few tunes.

He then went back to his Mercedes and returned with two sods of turf which he presented to Mick O'Connell, the famous Kerry footballer who was an Independent councillor. Micko then went off and came back with his own turf, making a reciprocal presentation to the Kilgarvan man, to great amusement all round. There was regular banter between the duo at council meetings and O'Connell was one of the first to tell Healy-Rae that he would do better as an Independent.

The other side to Healy-Rae was that he could hector and bully his way through meetings when he wanted to raise an issue, or force something through. He could shout louder than anybody else and, when needed, had a tongue that could scorch paint off walls. "If you came into this world with only a shovel in your hand, you'd die of starvation," was his withering

Jackie Healy-Rae, right, pictured, in Tralee, with Nobel Peace Prize winner
Dr Sean MacBride and Cllr Dick Spring, later to become Tanaiste and leader
of the Labour party, during Healy-Rae's tenure as chairman of Kerry County
Council, in 1980/'81. (Kennelly photo)

put-down to a rival councillor during a heated debate one day.

Healy-Rae was a regular at the Fianna Fáil Ard Fheis and often spoke
at the gathering, which helped give him a profile with party members
countrywide. He was also the centre of the social side of the Ard Fheis.
One night, things were a bit quiet in the Burlington Hotel, so a few of the
Kerry attendees went to him and asked him if he could organise some craic.
According to John O'Donoghue, from Farranfore, Jackie spontaneously
thumped a table with his fist, saying he would sort things.

It was about 11 o'clock and he got on the phone. Soon after, Dermot
O'Brien, the singer and musician who had played previously in the bar in
Kilgarvan, arrived. Jackie had phoned him at home in Dublin. The hotel
provided a room for a party, people flooded in and some few lads collected
money at the door. Fianna Fáil changed the rules after that – so that only
the party could organise such shindigs in the future.

Healy-Rae did not direct the June 1981 and February 1982 general elections, in Kerry South, but showed his ambitions in Fianna Fáil were still very much alive when he unsuccessfully contested the Senate elections. He narrowly lost the election to the Upper House, claiming he did not get the support he deserved from the party. Neither did he get all the votes he had been promised, he claimed. Healy-Rae was back as director of elections for the 1987 election in which O'Leary and O'Donoghue were successful. O'Donoghue had been defeated in three previous elections.

Healy-Rae, who had been director of elections in several campaigns, caused some surprise when he indicated he would not be seeking the role for the 1992 general election. Though he didn't say it publicly, the belief in Fianna Fáil was that he was disappointed at not getting a Taoiseach's nomination to the Senate.

John O'Leary says he tried to get Charlie Haughey to nominate Healy-Rae, in 1989, but Haughey's reply was the party already had a senator, Tom Fitzgerald, of Dingle, in the constituency. Fitzgerald was a close friend of Haughey's and, as long as he was there, there was no room for anyone else. In 1992, O'Donoghue and O'Leary (for the last time) retained their Dáil seats.

— 3 —

Holding Forth on Issues Gripping the Nation

A decade before the GAA - after much internal wrangling and bitterness - decided to open Croke Park to soccer and rugby, Jackie Healy-Rae believed it was 'pure, sheer nonsense' to confine the GAA headquarters to Gaelic games. Though a former player and follower of hurling and football, he had no time for the narrow, deep-rooted conservatism of the GAA which, he felt, was as damaging to the country as any adverse, outside influence could be.

A populist politician he might have been, but neither would it have been unusual for him to go against the prevailing public mood on issues. One of the contradictions in Jackie Healy-Rae.

Soon after the scandal involving his friend, Bishop Eamon Casey, who fathered a son with an American divorcee, Annie Murphy, was exposed, Healy-Rae made it clear he was not among those castigating Casey. Furthermore, he was disappointed at the censorious attitude adopted by many people at the time. Too much was being made of revelations about the bishop's sex life, he protested. "It hurt me. Eamon Casey was a very personal, great friend of mine."

Nor did he agree with some of Casey's episcopal colleagues that the errant bishop, who had fled the country, should be cast out forever. Bring the man back, for God's sake, was his mantra.

His surprisingly liberal views on a smorgasbord of popular issues were vented in what was, arguably, one of the best interviews he ever gave. Liam Fay, of the *Hot Press* magazine, a publication largely about young people's favoured music, travelled to Killarney, in May 1995, to meet the 'big

32

Bishop Eamon Casey, whom Healy-Rae supported, pictured outside his old home in Firies, in 1969. (© macmonagle.com)

man', as if he were referring to Ian Paisley, the hardline unionist firebrand in Northern Ireland. Jackie stood at about 5 feet 7 inches and was quite pleasant and forthcoming when he sat down with the journalist in a town centre hotel. He was by now the country's best-known Fianna Fáil councillor, still loyal to the party and some distance away from his election as an independent TD.

The pair got the frivolity out of the way early on. Fay was curious about Jackie's much-talked of crossover hairstyle, as well as his range of hats and caps. There were about a dozen, astrakhan-style Russian hats, worn to funerals and other formal occasions, he revealed. When fooling around at home, any headgear at all would do, while the trademark, tartan flat cap was donned when going out in the general sense.

There was a lot of idle talk at the time that Jackie was wearing a wig, so he challenged Fay to put £50 on the table as a bet. "Here's your chance. But, if I'm not wearing a wig, you'll go home and I'll have your fifty quid in my pocket." Fay left his money in his pocket. Wisely.

Tonsorial matters dispensed with, they got down to the more serious business during what the interviewer described as 'an appointment with chaos' and a meeting with the Kingdom's Kingmaker, whom he described as the Cardinal Richelieu of The MacGillycuddy's Reeks. Their encounter was, typically, squeezed in between an unexpected Southern Health Board engagement, trouble with the engine of an excavating machine at home and a Fianna Fáil meeting that night.

Jackie talked of meeting all Fianna Fáil taoisigh. He had got as far as shaking hands with the first of these, Eamon de Valera, during a visit to Kerry by Dev and had become more familiar with several of the others. (His later dealings Bertie Ahern and Brian Cowen, whose governments he supported, were still down the road).

Something he made clear was that he had no time for Albert Reynolds as Taoiseach or leader of Fianna Fáil. Nor would he give Reynolds any credit for his work in the Peace Process, in Northern Ireland. "There's people praising Reynolds over the Peace Process thing. My honest humble opinion is that whatever Fianna Fáil man was at the helm at that particular time, or whoever from whatever party was at the helm, they'd have achieved the exact same thing as the Peace Process. All the people were sick of it (the years of conflict). Politicians were sick of it. The IRA were sick of it."

An implacable opponent of Reynolds, who succeeded Charlie Haughey as Taoiseach and Fianna Fáil leader, Healy-Rae once dubbed him as a 'disaster' and refused to attend the party's 1993 Ard Fheis, which was a strong protest for him, because of the manner in which Haughey was ousted by Reynolds.

It should not come as a surprise that Jackie and Bishop Casey were friends. Both were alike in personality – effervescent, humorous, excellent communicators, and having egos that needed to be continually massaged by public attention and acclaim. Men with a definite human touch.

In 1992, when *The Irish Times* broke the story that the then Bishop of Galway had fathered a son, the nation was stunned. To say that people were scandalised, flabbergasted, breathless and disbelieving would not overstate the situation. To this day, some people maintain it was a significant watermark in the decline of the Catholic Church in Ireland. Slippage, however, had started as far back as the 1960's and the revelations of clerical child sex abuse that were to the come in the decades following Casey's much-publicised indiscretion put his sin in a lower category of scandal, it might be argued.

However, the Casey/Murphy story of forbidden love and broken rules captivated the nation for a long time and still gets occasional airings. Their son, Peter, was in his teens when it all became public. The bishop fled to New York and later spent five years as a missionary in Ecuador. That only added to the sense of banishment felt by his admirers. To many people, the worst part of the story was that he had used diocesan funds for the upkeep and education of Peter in the US.

While the Church did not encourage his return to Ireland, public opinion was divided on whether he should be welcomed back. Healy-Rae remained unequivocal in his support. As time went on and much-worse scandals emerged in the Church, attitudes towards the bishop softened. In 2006, he eventually returned and worked in the parish of Shanaglish, Co Galway. Now in his late eighties, he is suffering from Alzheimer's Disease and is in a nursing home.

Casey's downfall was in sharp contrast to the adulation he had received in the 1960's. Born in Firies, Co Kerry, in 1927, Casey returned like a hero to Kerry as bishop in 1969. Bands played, flags were unfurled and corks popped. Everywhere he went, crowds came out to greet him. He ruled the church there until his transfer to Galway as bishop in 1976.

Prior to being appointed to Kerry, Casey had an outstanding record as a priest in London where he did sterling work in housing needy people and in other areas concerning emigrant welfare. He also became a media personality and was regularly on TV chat shows, with Gay Byrne on the Late Late Show for instance. In short, he was a celebrity cleric who hit Kerry like a proverbial tsunami. Enjoying pop star status, admirers turned up wherever he appeared, including many young people.

As Healy-Rae would say, Casey was a mighty man for attending functions and enjoying a few drinks with people. He could often be heard blasting out songs - *Come Back Paddy Reilly* was a favourite - and urging a chorus to join in towards the end of an evening. A huge contrast to what the faithful in Kerry had been accustomed to. Their idea of a bishop was a rather austere, aloof and pious figure like Casey's predecessor Bishop Denis Moynihan. But the people, and Healy-Rae, took this singing, joking, hail-fellow-well-met bishop to their hearts.

Jackie was drawn to him straight away and they met at events such as fleadhanna cheoil, where music and drink went hand in hand.

Though a light drinker himself, Jackie noticed the bishop enjoyed a tipple or two and said if the man had a single weakness, it was that he might have the few extra. When asked if he had been aware of the dalliance with Annie Murphy, Healy-Rae replied he did not know of it. But when the story broke, he added, he knew drink was the cause of the problem. In the best Irish tradition, drink was the demon, he believed.

"I knew the man inside out. Sometime on or about the time he got into difficulty with her, I opened a fleadh cheoil in Castlemaine and a fantastic fleadh cheoil it was. I was the chairman of Kerry County Comhaltas Ceoltoiri Eireann and had only finished speaking to this big crowd of musicians when who arrives in his big flash car than only (bishop) Eamon Casey."

To make a long story short, they had a long night and an amount of drink was quaffed. And if Casey had a good few that night, he had good few other nights as well, Jackie reckoned, further concluding that it was the drinking that led him to his difficulties with Annie Murphy. Casey was a fine, decent honourable man, he should come back to Ireland and he should never have been pushed out, according to Jackie.

Jackie's views on the so-called liberal agenda were somewhat mixed and unclear, but always his own. The way he saw the abortion issue was if people wanted to go to England they would go, no matter what the government told them.

On divorce, he felt that if two people cannot continue living together and decide to break up and go their separate ways, they are going to do it no matter what law anyone makes. In his view, there was too much of a focus on such issues in a country which had plenty of other problems to deal with, and not to be getting involved in people's personal lives.

By the 1990's in Ireland, unmarried people were commonly cohabiting and the result of a referendum on divorce would not make an iota of difference, only 'vexate' people without changing what was happening on the ground, he opined. The divorce ban was lifted in a November 1995 referendum.

Taking a somewhat harder line on abortion, he said it was his considered opinion abortion took away life and he did not like it at all. "If there was abortion in this country, would it incite more of them to have it done? I don't know. I could be very wrong. It's a very hard question, but all the talk in the world isn't going to stop a person having an abortion if that's what they've decided."

He did not seem to have any issue with contraception and had a condom dispensing machine installed in the male toilet of his pub in the early 1990's. One day a customer was perplexed when he went to the machine for cigarettes and saw these strange packets that had never before been put on public view in Kilgarvan. Never heard of the brand Durex before. Funny-looking cigarettes? Unsure, the man asked a barmaid why the cigarette machine was put in the toilet.

Quick thinking and barely hiding a smirk, she replied it was because the fags were cheaper in the toilet than in the bar! The innocent man hadn't a clue what was in the machine and kicked up an awful racket, Jackie recalled with a mischievous laugh.

Jackie died prior to the same same-sex marriage referendum, in 2015, in which his sons, Michael, his successor a TD, and Danny, a county councillor, voted No to gay marriage. Danny's son, Johnny, also a councillor, indicated he was voting Yes, however.

It's hard to know what way Jackie would have gone. His previous views on the subject were very much in line with public opinion some years earlier in Ireland. He had professed a dislike of homosexuality, while pointing out that he, the government or anyone else could do nothing about it. "It's too powerful for all them people," he held forth. Given the growing acceptance of homosexuality as a reality in life, he would probably have become more tolerant of it, but actually voting in support of same sex marriage may have been a step too far for him.

On religion, he had a simple philosophy – do what you can to help people and don't do anyone any harm. "My head isn't lost over religion. I'd be very sympathetic to people who're in difficulty of any kind and always have been. Those kind of practicalities are better than the auld pious thing of which there has been far too much in this country down the years. It's (piety) thin on the ground now though , and that's a very good thing."

———————————•———————————

As outlined in a previous chapter, his links with the GAA went back to boyhood, but the rules of the association were not always to his liking. As well as a ban on playing 'foreign' games in GAA grounds and on GAA members attending such games elsewhere, there was also a ban on 'foreign' music at GAA events. Only Irish or ceili music was permitted at dances and other social functions run by the GAA.

Around 1960, Kilgarvan GAA club was short of funds and decided to hold a dance to bring in a few pounds. Jackie, then a leading light in the club, took a bold step. He booked a Dublin big band, under Ralph Sylvester, and the Carnegie Ballroom, in nearby Kenmare. But he had to get around GAA rules in case zealots tried to stymie him. The GAA had vigilantes, some called them spies, at the time who would report on people who broke the rules. So he made the booking under the Kilgarvan Sports Committee because a lot of GAA people 'were going mad about this jazz band'.

In any case, a huge crowd turned up. The dance was hailed a success and made more money for the GAA 'than they ever realised before on one night of their lives, or ever will again'. The episode showed a facility for getting around hard and fast rules, something that would serve him well throughout his political life during which pragmatism and practicality ruled. Even if laws were set in stone, he knew he could find a way around them – almost always!

He never agreed with keeping Croke Park exclusively for GAA games and was also firmly against the GAA ban on members of the security forces in the North playing hurling and football. On keeping soccer and rugby out, he had this say: "There isn't a question or a shadow of doubt about it. At present, I feel this confining of Croke Park to Gaelic games is pure, sheer nonsense. "'Tis absolutely ridiculous, to put it mildly. We're all Irishmen and we all have the spirit of the Irish. We all helped to put Croke Park where it is. Every one of us that played and got our hands and legs broken and our heads split several times."

As for the ban on members of the police force in the North and the British army, he had this to say: "Pure, sheer nonsense too. Absolutely ridiculous! I'd leave every bloody man play whatever game he wants and no more about it. Soccer is a fantastic game, hurling is a wonderful game and, of course, football is a great game."

In November 2001, the GAA decided by an overwhelming majority to abolish its controversial Rule 21, which banned members of

MEP Sean Kelly – the GAA opened up Croke Park to rugby and soccer during his tenure as president of the association, which Healy-Rae strongly supported.
(© macmonagle.com)

the British security forces and police from membership of the association. The decision was seen as a significant boost to the Peace Process as the way had now been paved for young men and women who played Gaelic games to join the British Army and the Police Service of Northern Ireland (PSNI), which replaced the RUC.

In April 2005, the GAA, under the presidency of another Kerryman, Sean Kelly, decided, again overwhelmingly, to remove the notorious Rule 42 thereby opening Croke Park to rugby and soccer. Kelly, who had campaigned vigorously for the rule's removal, subsequently entered politics and is currently in his second term as a Fine Gael member of the European Parliament for the Ireland South constituency. Like many another former leading GAA player or official who had successfully entered the political arena, Kelly used his training in the GAA - which some observers regard as a political-type organisation - to good effect. After all, it did take a deal of political skill and lobbying various power groups in the GAA to get rid of Rule 42.

On February 24, 2007, a crowd gathered to watch a match on television in Healy-Rae's bar in the GAA stronghold of Kilgarvan. No run-of-the-mill match this - the first rugby international between Ireland and England to be played in Croke Park.

There were reminders from banner-waving protestors outside Croke Park about the Bloody Sunday atrocity on the hallowed sod, in November, 1920. Fourteen people were shot dead by British troops on the occasion of a Dublin versus Tipperary football match, an act of retaliation for the IRA's killing of British agents in Dublin that morning. But Healy-Rae was happy about staging the rugby game in the crucible that was GAA headquarters on another historic day, in 2007.

The change in attitude and atmosphere from that murderous day 87 years previously could hardly have been more pronounced. It also signalled

Queen Elizabeth II at the English Market, in Cork. Healy-Rae welcomed her 2011 state visit to Ireland, but had mixed views previously on royal visits. (© Valerie O'Sullivan)

a new era in relations between the old enemies, with peace in the North et al. Many in the 80,000-plus capacity crowd were clearly emotional and in tears as they stood for the national anthems, Amhran na bFhiann and God Save The Queen. A few dichard GAA people are still opposed to soccer and rugby in Croke Park and some have not gone back there since then in protest. But the great majority and Jackie Healy-Rae had no problems with it.

Healy-Rae also welcomed the four-day, state visit of Queen Elizabeth 11 to Ireland, in May 2011. Sixteen years before that, he had voiced inconsistent views on such visits, which did not meet with unanimous agreement politically.

There were Sinn Fein protests in Dublin when Prince Charles became the first member of the British royal family to visit the state, on May 31, 1995. His great-uncle, Lord Louis Mountbatten, had been killed with three others in an IRA explosion while holidaying in Mullaghmore, Co Sligo, in August 1979, and the passage of time had not fully healed the wounds.

There was tight security for the prince's one-day visit and not everybody came out to welcome him. But Healy-Rae could see nothing wrong with the visit, declaring: "All belonging to us went over to England and I'd welcome any people from England to come over here. There should be no problem about it, only welcome the bloody man over there and that's that." That showed a contradictory side of Healy-Rae who, earlier in 1995, opposed a suggested state visit by the Queen to mark the 150th anniversary of the Famine because Britain 'gave no help whatsoever' when thousands of Irish people were dying of starvation.

Also, he believed Britain should pull out of the North and leave Ireland her 32 counties. "They (Britain) have enough irons in the fire not to be stuck in Ireland. What I'm hoping for is that I'll still be around when the people of the North will see the light and the majority will opt to join the 32 counties. And I want that to happen by peaceful means."

One of his wishes not yet fulfilled.

— 4 —

The Split

"You won't let me down," he pleads, all twinkle from under the tartan and thrusting out one big hand. "Not at all," replies the voter, mesmerised by the smallish man with the biggest charisma. "Thanks very, very much," he says, clapping the laughing voter on the back. Off he goes up the street pressing more flesh, thumping more backs. On road to Dáil Éireann. Full on.

When the long-serving Fianna Fáil TD for Kerry South, John O'Leary, announced, in September 1996, he would not be fighting the general election due in the summer of 1997, the succession race began immediately in the party. And Jackie Healy-Rae was in the field.

The convention to choose candidates was fixed for October 27, 1996. In the time-honoured tradition of dynastic politics, the retiring deputy's son, Brian, who had been co-opted to Kerry County Council only a few months before, was confidently expected to succeed his father. But nobody, not least John O'Leary, was surprised that Healy-Rae was about to grasp an opportunity he had been seeking for much of his political life. From the start of the convention campaign, O'Leary Senior knew Healy-Rae would be Brian's toughest opponent.

In his memoir, the deputy described it as rough, hard-fought campaign from the start. He accused some Healy-Rae supporters of 'sniping' at Brian from the word go. He advised Brian to focus on his own campaign and not get into arguments with his rivals. "I don't think that Healy-Rae's behaviour before the 1996 convention was anything personal against me, or Brian," he recalled. "It wasn't a regular feature of his character, but he could be belligerent and there was no arguing with him sometimes. He had a gang of supporters with him and they were a tough lot and reminded me a bit of Charlie Haughey's supporters around the Dáil in the early 1980's."

At the convention in the Gleneagle Hotel, Killarney, Deputy John O'Donoghue was automatically given the nod. In the contest, Brian O'Leary finished first on 144 votes, followed by Healy-Rae on 94, with Tom Fleming on 45 and Tom Doherty on 39. So, Brian O'Leary was to be the second candidate. After the convention, Jackie and his advisers decided to seek a meeting with Bertie Ahern. Their aim was to get him added to the Fianna Fáil ticket in Kerry South.

They were welcomed to Leinster House, on February 14, by the Taoiseach-elect Ahern and Jackie listed all the things he had done for the party over many years. Furthermore, he warned Fianna Fáil would lose one of its two seats in Kerry South if it did not have a third candidate.

As their meeting ended, Jackie made an earnest, personal request to Bertie. "Don't put me down the road as an independent candidate. Please give me a chance to run and I'll be faithful to you." In Jackie's words, however,

Getting their posters up during the 1997 campaign, outside Killarney. Jackie and Michael Healy-Rae. (© macmonagle.com)

Bertie was about to 'to make the biggest blunder' of his life. Bertie assured him he did not wish to see him break from Fianna Fáil and Jackie would be hearing from him following an imminent meeting of the party's election strategy committee, in Dublin.

Jackie and Maurice Galvin stepped back onto the Kerry train at Heuston Station almost certain he would be on the Fianna Fáil ticket. Speculation on the intentions of the Healy-Rae camp continued, meanwhile, as Jackie continue to play a persuasion game to be added.

There were also firm indications from senior levels in Fianna Fáil, and from the O'Donoghue and O'Leary camps, the two-candidate strategy would not be changed. It was clear the O'Donoghue and O'Leary dynasties and party strategists didn't want him on the ticket. PJ Mara, Charlie Haughey's former spokesman and adviser, was Fianna Fáil's national director of elections and he was also adamant no candidate would be added. Showing some disdain, Healy-Rae came to know the sartorially-elegant Mara as 'the man with the top coat'.

Only to be expected then that Healy-Rae should call a council of war, to be attended by his nearest and dearest. Denis P O'Sullivan, long-time postmaster in Kilgarvan, a friend, neighbour and fellow hurler, who has also since died, recalled such an event for this writer after the 1997 election. He had a visit from Jackie on a Monday night some weeks prior to the election. Jackie told him that, since the convention, many people had been urging him to enter the contest and the time had come to make up his mind, one way or the other.

Some Healy-Rae family members from around the country were summonsed to Kilgarvan for a discussion and a decision. Denis P said he and Maurice Galvin were the only non-family members present, with Jackie asking him to come along to act as a chairman and to get a full, common sense discussion going.

Family members had their say; there were mixed opinions and Jackie listened more than he spoke. The financial implications; the high level of organisation required, time and work involved, not to mention the seriousness of breaking from an established party and the uphill battle an Independent would face, were all debated.

A detailed report on contacts with Fianna Fáil headquarters in Dublin was also given and news of an offer was still awaited. "Rightly or wrongly, I got the distinct impression that if Dublin made contact announcing that there would not be a third candidate, but that they would give him a vigorous push for the Senate, he would have accepted," wrote Denis P. "I realise that he could not be guaranteed a (Senate) seat without Fianna Fáil becoming the government, which remained a strong possibility. One way or another, it should be attainable."

At the end of a lengthy discussion, it was decided that further contact would be made with Dublin within a few days and that the launching of Jackie's campaign as an Independent should be postponed for a week. "This was agreed on. The rest is history. Apparently, there was no contact from Dublin and, by the weekend, it was well and widely known that the launching would go ahead at Scott's Hotel (Killarney), on the following Wednesday night," noted Denis P.

The Healy-Raes had obviously given up on hearing from Fianna Fáil, in Dublin. The continuing line from the party was that Jackie should give his full support to the two nominated candidates, as he had always done. According to the Healy-Raes, the next they heard from Mr Ahern was when Jackie's vote was needed to secure the formation of a Fianna Fáil/Progressive Democrats Coalition.

Jackie claimed to be 'flabbergasted' at the lack of communication on his request to be added to the ticket. The die was cast and he started to prepare for the biggest solo run of his life. He immediately set about contacting his many friends in Fianna Fáil in the constituency, including Teddy O'Connor, of Killorglin, son of former Fianna Fáil TD Timothy (Chub) O'Connor, and key supporters who had backed him as a county councillor and canvassed for him in numerous elections.

Paudie O'Callaghan, of the Failte Hotel, Killarney, whose family and the Healy-Raes are close friends, had proposed Healy-Rae for a nomination at the Fianna Fáil convention. He said they knew Healy-Rae would not get through and were banking on Bertie adding him to the ticket. But there was a clear hint from Healy-Rae, at the end of the convention, when he tapped the microphone and said he might be knocking on doors yet!

At a meeting in Scott's Hotel, on April 9, Healy-Rae announced he would be an Independent Fianna Fáil candidate, but he would not be resigning from the party. It was up to the party to sack him, as was the rule if he stood against nominated candidates. Launching his campaign with typical dash, he warned Ahern and O'Donoghue would 'dance to my music' before it was all over.

"He had his own mind made up, especially when Bertie didn't give him an answer straight away," Paudie O'Callaghan recalled. "I remember him saying downstairs in The Failte, 'I'm going solo'. It was the only time he had a chance to go and it was a crazy campaign from start to finish, changing from hour to hour. I spent a lot of time canvassing with him and keeping up with him was an ordeal. He was jumping over hedges! The campaign gathered momentum as it went along, with more volunteers joining in and an ever-growing, feel good factor."

So, the big break with Fianna Fáil had come. Some leading lights dismissed Healy-Rae and what they saw as bluster from him. They were saying he'd be hard put to get the 2,000 number ones he polled in the previous local elections. They were being smug at their peril. The man with the knuckle-crunching handshake knew the constituency better than most; every cumann, crossroads and Fianna Fáil officer of note. He also had an intimate knowledge of the register of electors.

He played on being 'badly treated' by Fianna Fáil after all his years of service to the party while, at the same time, pitching for the Fianna Fáil vote. Importantly, he succeeded in bringing a significant number of party stalwarts with him and they were crucial to his campaign. The constituency was stirring. "You won't let me down," was heard thousands of times as he canvassed voters. His entry to the race added life and colour to the election scene, in Kerry South. What looked like being a predictable, boring constituency became one of the most interesting in the country.

Healy-Rae would use all his experience and contacts in an all-out bid to win one of the three seats, saying he'd be in every nook and corner looking for votes. He also warned Fianna Fáil was in grave danger of losing one of its two seats and said it was as a result of pressure from his supporters he decided to run. The decision to leave the party was the hardest he had ever made, and with regret, he stated.

He had already established his election headquarters in Scott's Hotel, owned by leading Killarney hotelier Maurice O'Donoghue, while another Killarney Fianna Fáil town councillor, Dermot O'Callaghan, of the Failte Hotel, threw in his lot with Healy-Rae.

O'Donoghue, also owner of the Gleneagle Hotel, had previously broken ranks with Fianna Fáil and got himself elected as an Independent town councillor before later returning to the party fold. A highly influential figure and a big employer, O'Donoghue was, at least, sympathetic to Healy-Rae and they were also good friends. The O'Callaghan family was actively involved in the campaign and the early omens were encouraging.

Michael Healy-Rae, not yet a councillor, was appointed director of elections. All the issues in their campaign were local – roads, jobs, farming, fishing, housing and health. Jackie also claimed the constituency had been grossly neglected and he was the man to put all that right. The fact that he was so well known made it easy for himself and his canvassers on the doorsteps and his gregarious, outgoing personality was used to good effect.

People like Killarney man Kevin Tarrant, who had never before been in an election campaign, joined in. Tarrant worked on their campaign literature, advertising and communications. While the vast majority of candidates were still relying on fax machines, this campaign was using email which was quite new at the time. The message being put out was that Healy-Rae would create a right racket when he got into that 'big house above in Dublin' and would be a voice for the people.

As might be expected, the campaign attracted a barrage of publicity and he knew how to exploit every media opportunity presented by the colour writers. "Jackie Healy-Rae has all the angles covered. He wears two watches, one on each wrist, just in case one of them stops. They are not battery or wind-up watches, he said. They get their energy from his arm movements. There's no danger that either will stop in the next week," observed Catherine Cleary in *The Irish Times*.

ELECTION OFFICE, COLLEGE STREET, KILLARNEY, Co. KERRY.
TEL. 064 - 37233

Main Street, Kilgarvan, Co. Kerry.
Tel. 064 - 85315

Since I declared as a candidate for the General Election these are the issues the people of Killarney have expressed most concern about.

1. TRAFFIC CONGESTION

As Killarney is Ireland's premier tourist destination we deserve a better road system. I am calling for immediate implementation of:

A) The inner relief road from New Street carpark to the Golden Gates.

B) The outer relief road from the Tralee road to Ballydowney Bridge.

C) The outer relief road from the Cathedral to Ross road to Flesk Bridge on the Muckross road.

Local residential roads like the Mill Road, Woodlawn Road and the Countess Road are not the answer to this problem.

2. JOBS

Since the closure of "Pretty Polly" very few new industrial jobs have been created. Many people are now travelling long distances to find work. We require a significant new industry for Killarney to re-open the "Pretty Polly" gates. We must also work to extend the tourist season in Killarney.

3. HOUSING

There is an acute shortage of Local Authority Housing to meet the growing demand. I am calling again on Killarney U.D.C. and Kerry County Council to provide land banks to meet this need as a matter of urgency. The proper planning and development of the Killarney area is of paramount importance to me.

The protection and enhancement of the environment and the creation of viable opportunities for the young people to live and make a living in their home area is my great concern.

Therefore I appeal for **YOUR No. 1 VOTE** and your total support to ensure I can deliver on all these issues.

IT'S TIME SOUTH KERRY HAD A VOICE TO BE HEARD IN DÁIL EIREANN

Jackie Healy-Rae

A key election worker, John O'Donoghue, of Farranfore, could see support growing as the campaign went on. "I was very confident he was going to be elected," recalled O'Donoghue. "Many people from Fianna Fáil went with him and he was conducting a tremendous campaign. He had a way about him that took the seriousness out of politics and brought a bit of fun to the whole thing."

It was a campaign that blended old-style electioneering and modern-day tactics. He could be found at after-Mass meetings outside rural churches, standing on milk crates or a trailer, preaching fire and brimstone, or dancing with young people in Killarney nightclubs. Youth identified with him and saw him as a novelty, quirky candidate. Because of his cap, he was being compared in nightclubs to the tartan-clad Bay City Rollers, a popular boy band of yesteryear. But he was deadly serious about his business and utterly determined to get elected.

As polling day neared, the tempo was raised. On the eve of polling, thousands of leaflets urging a final push behind Healy-Rae were dropped into letter boxes and handed out in Killarney. Business cards with a helpline and letters had been widely circulated in the previous fortnight.

ABOVE: Almost over the hill.
A leaflet circulated a few days before polling.
OPPOSITE: An election leaflet from 1997.

Timely, well-thought out advertisements were placed in local newspapers. On the big day, the Healy-Raes had their people on the ground everywhere and a transport system to ensure all supporters got to the booths to do their democratic duty.

It was a remarkable, poll-topping performance. Healy-Rae had made the most of being let loose as an Independent, using all his personality and charm to woo voters. At 25, Fine Gael's Aidan O'Connor was the youngest candidate. At 66, Healy-Rae was the oldest. Looking back, O'Connor reckons the vast majority of people read it all wrong about Jackie in the run-up to the election. Unless someone was on the hustings every day, they could be

---

GENERAL ELECTION, JUNE 6, 1997, KERRY SOUTH, FIRST COUNT (QUOTA: 8,875)

Healy-Rae, Jackie (Ind) 7,220
O'Donoghue, John (Fianna Fáil) 7,204
Moynihan Cronin, Breeda (Labour) 4,998
MacGearailt, Breandan (Fianna Fáil) 4,172
O'Leary, Brian (Fianna Fáil) 4,079
O'Connor, Aidan (Fine Gael) 3,041
Kelly, Jim (Fine Gael) 1,847
Cronin, PJ (Ind) 1,557
Gleeson, Michael (SKIA) 1,388

RESULT: Healy-Rae and O'Donoghue (5th count), Moynihan Cronin (7th count).

---

forgiven for thinking that he was no more than a renegade councillor who broke away from Fianna Fáil with a bitter taste in his mouth.

"Nothing could be further from the truth," said O'Connor, currently a journalist with *Kerry's Eye* newspaper, Tralee, and a respected writer on political affairs. "Jackie had gone where no one had ever gone before: nooks and crannies of a sprawling constituency that I couldn't spell, never mind canvass. He was the culmination of almost 40 years of political campaigning. He knew the register of electors better than his own family. He knew where there was a vote and where there was an idle promise."

While Fine Gael were bogged down in internal wrangling, the Healy-Rae machine gathered pace. What to some appeared like a bit of fun out of Kilgarvan quickly turned into a slick, methodical campaign. The spin getting through to voters was that it was Fianna Fáil that had left Healy-Rae - not the other way round. This man of pension age wanted one chance to get to Leinster House and needed the support of the people. The campaign was presidential, built around the candidate's magnetic personality, something that was continued in subsequent elections.

As O'Connor was driving home to Rathmore late one Saturday night during the campaign, he received a phone call saying he needed to be in a Killarney nightclub straight away. Slightly taken aback, he asked why. He was informed Jackie was on the dance floor which was full of teenagers, all wearing Jackie Healy-Rae election badges and thoroughly enjoying this highly original character, three or four times their age.

"He was bringing fun to politics. When I was told that the deejay handed him the microphone in the packed nightclub, I knew the ball was burst. Game over. All around the housing estates, children chanted, 'Jackie Healy-Rae, Jackie Healy-Rae'. Their moms and dads thought it was all a bit of fun. Fine Gael election strategists told me to ignore it. Children don't have a vote, they said. Poor advice. Children influence parents more than any other group."

Jackie was at his best when speech-making outside churches after weekend Masses, according to O'Connor who was a first-hand witness to these theatrical performances. He was like a man possessed bursting to get to Dáil Éireann where he would put things right for the constituency. O'Connor, nevertheless, said he fought cleanly and did not resort to dirty political tactics. But he had subtle ways of putting opponents down. Outside Glenflesk church, he offered the youthful O'Connor the honour to speak first which was accepted – only to be regretted afterwards.

"Delighted with my performance and applause, Jackie was straight up

Jackie Healy-Rae being shouldered high by supporters after being elected at a count in Killarney. (© macmonagle.com)

on the trailer and told the faithful that he was delighted there were 'some young fellas trying their hand at the Dáil' before telling them that he was in politics long before I was only 'a small little child in nappies at the foot of the kitchen table'. If I was small in childhood, I felt even smaller then!" The callow youth was no match for the battle-tested, old pro.

O'Connor firmly believes more young people voted for Jackie in 1997 than for any other candidate. And the reason, in O'Connor's opinion? He was fresh and brought something new; promising the 'sun, moon and stars' and making a better hand at delivering all three than anybody else.

The irony of the election was that O'Connor had been expected to scoop the so-called young vote and Healy-Rae the grey vote. But the Fine Gael post-election analysis concluded the opposite happened. Two weeks before polling day, O'Connor was certain Healy-Rae was going to be elected. All the talk in the housing estates and along boreens leading to one-off houses in scattered country areas was about Healy-Rae. The older man had the whole place lit up, according to O'Connor.

There's a picture of Jackie talking into O'Connor's ear at the election count in Killarney. A picture that tells a story. "When thousands turned up to celebrate his victory, Jackie took time to call me aside. In true style, he gripped my arm, squeezed hard and held on. 'Don't be down in yourself one bit, garsun,' I remember him saying into my ear. 'You nearly did the devil altogether'. That was Jackson."

At the time, former Tanaiste Dick Spring, who was re-elected as a Labour TD for Kerry North, noted with interest what was happening in the neighbouring constituency. Like many other people, he believed Fianna Fáil made a major mistake in allowing Healy-Rae leave the party and also underestimated him. Had he been added to the Fianna Fáil ticket, there wouldn't have been the sympathy factor and Fianna Fáil would have retained its two seats, in Spring's opinion.

Healy-Rae and his supporters celebrated for several days and nights. The man himself became a celebrity and was unable to cope with invitations to all kind of functions from hen parties, to stag parties, birthday parties, photographic sessions with models, shop and pub openings. His phones were hopping and he was on guest lists everywhere. All great fun and a sort of honeymoon period.

But, away from the eyes of the public, there was serious business to be done. He was compiling a 'shopping list' of things that needed to be done in the constituency. To the forefront of his mind was his, or Bertie Ahern's, next move. As Fianna Fáil and the Progressive Democrats (PDs) had not won a majority, there would be a hung Dáil. Fianna Fáil had 77 seats and the PDs four, so Bertie needed the votes of at least two Independents to form a minority Fianna Fáil/PD administration. Healy-Rae and other Independents would be the power brokers and Bertie needed their support. They would have an opportunity to prop up a new government and secure deals for their constituencies.

Healy-Rae had the guile and experience to take full advantage of Bertie's dilemma. He had warned Fianna Fáil it would lose a seat in Kerry South if he wasn't added to the ticket and had been proved right. As he had signalled, Bertie and Fianna Fáil would have to reckon with him and, now, he was in a position of strength.

Jackie cracks the whip in readiness for Ahern's call

by Declan Colley

"I'll TAKE the whip from no man," Jackie Healy-Rae intoned with the intensity of a man actually facing the cat 'o' nine tails. "I have a lisht here," he said brandishing a blank piece of paper "and, until these demands are met, I'll be considering my position."

The hat-bedecked fireball from Kilgarvan laid down the law for any parliamentary alliance with typical candour and was cheered to the echo of a loyal throng.

Against the odds and embarrassingly for the party which dumped him, Jackie Healy Rae, triumphed in spectacular fashion in South Kerry.

From the moment the boxes were opened at the Great Southern Hotel count centre, it was obvious he was going places. "I was blackguarded out of a nomination at the convention," he claimed shortly after the vote sorting began, "but they'll be dancing to my music yet."

How right he was. By 1 pm, when the final tallies came through, it was clear the multi-faceted Healy-Rea was going to top the poll against the favourite, John O'Donoghue.

Even before the first official count had begun, his supporters were lauding "Deputy Healy Rae."

"I have hauled the highways and byways in this campaign and it looks like we'll be banging a few tables in Dublin with the support we got.

"On Thursday night 80 people knocked on 3,500 doors and gave out 3,500 leaflets in an hour. That's massive. No other party came close to having that sort of organisation."

If Fianna Fáil expect him simply to row in with them, however, they are in for a shock. "If that's what they think is going to happen, they're in for a surprise. We have been let down by the people who represented South Kerry and I'm going to put that right. South Kerry wanted me, but Fianna Fáil were not prepared to take me on. I was not afraid to take them on".

Could Bertie Ahern count on his support without pre-conditions? "He can whistle his ducks."

On June 11, five days after the election, Jackie travelled by train to Dublin. He was met at Heuston Station by Fianna Fáil Senator Donie Cassidy, who, in Puck Fair parlance, would become a tangler, or deal-broker, in upcoming talks with Bertie. Jackie sat into Cassidy's black Mercedes and was chauffeured to Leinster House.

The waiting media were curious. They wanted to know Healy-Rae's attitude and demeanour. Not for the first time, he surprised the reporters. "I'm the easiest man in the world to meet," he declared calmly. "They said I said Bertie would have to crawl to me. I'd never ask anyone to do that, not even a dog, and certainly not Bertie Ahern." There was no huffing and puffing and not a sign of belligerence from Healy-Rae. But he couldn't resist a little braggadocio. "Last Saturday was the proudest day of my life. I fought against the power of Fianna Fáil, Fine Gael and Labour and their massive funding and got 7,220 first preference votes."

He made it clear if he got a commitment from Ahern for investment in jobs and roads in south Kerry, the new government could rely on his vote. There was none of the wild talk about Ahern having to travel down to Kerry to meet him. Healy-Rae seemed the essence of reason and common sense. Everyone knew his support was crucial for the stability of the new government.

In an important gesture which recognised his Fianna Fáil background, he was given an office in a corridor exclusively for Fianna Fáil deputies. They were, essentially, saying he was still one of their own. Fianna Fáil top brass were taking him seriously. The 'buffoonery' for which he was portrayed in sections of the Dublin media and talk by Fine Gael's John Bruton that he was a character more at home in a Sean O'Casey play were forgotten.

When Taoiseach Charlie Haughey visited Kerry South during a general election campaign, in November 1982, Jackie Healy-Rae, as constituency director of elections for Fianna Fáil, joined in calls for a stable government. They wanted no more Gregorys, said Healy-Rae, a reference to a deal the Dublin Independent TD had done with Haughey, earlier that year,

OPPOSITE: How *The Examiner* reported the election victory, on its front page, June 9, 1997.

Former Taoiseach Bertie Ahern and Jackie Healy-Rae on the election trail.

in return for his support for a minority government. Under the Gregory Deal, there would be a multi-million pound regeneration of Dublin's north inner city.

However, in 1997, when Healy-Rae found himself in a similar position to Gregory, he had no problem about making a deal for his constituency. In the best political tradition, pragmatism took over. Just before the May 1997 election, he hinted he might be open to a Gregory-type deal. Campaigning in Killorglin, he said he intended to kick up 'holy bloody murder' in the Dáil over the dreadful state of roads in south Kerry and the lack of jobs in the county. "'Tis a sort of Gregory deal. If I hold the balance of power, I'd vote for Bertie Ahern if there was funding for the county roads and some guarantee of jobs for the young people," he told *The Irish Times*.

As expected, Bertie concluded agreements with Healy-Rae and two other Independents from the so-called Fianna Fáil gene pool - Harry Blaney, Donegal North East, and Mildred Fox, Wicklow, with another Independent, Tom Gildea, Donegal, also supporting. All got separate deals for their constituencies in return for pledges to vote with the Government.

Michael Healy-Rae, his sister Rosemary, a barrister, and an inner circle of advisers, including engineer Risteard O Lionaird and John O'Donoghue, Farranfore, were all part of the negotiating team. O Lionaird revealed, years later, that Fine Gael made an approach to Jackie offering him a Cabinet ministry in return for his support in the event of Fine Gael forming a government.

Fine Gael leader John Bruton, who had been Taoiseach in the previous Government, phoned Jackie from Newfoundland and found him to be very courteous. Agriculture was the suggested ministry for pensioner-cum-rookie TD. But, Fine Gael just didn't have the numbers to form a government and the deal with Bertie was a better and more sustainable fit.

The itemised, 'confidential' agreement with Ahern - details of which were not made public at the time - included a large number of road projects around the constituency, money for piers and harbours, grants for agriculture and pledges on job-creation. In the years ahead, Healy-Rae would make numerous announcements for the constituency which were included, either specifically or by aspiration, in the agreement.

Preparing what looks like a lengthy 'shopping list' for his negotiations with taoiseach-elect Bertie Ahern. (© macmonagle.com)

5

Settling into the Dáil

Supporters called it the Healy-Rae Special. As early as 7.30am, on Thursday June 26, 1997, they began to gather at Killarney Railway Station. It was the day they had all worked and waited for. The assembly of the 28th Dáil in which their man would play a prominent part. Spirits were high as the train approached and some were already humming the chorus, "Jackie Healy-Rae is on his way, Jackie Healy-Rae is here to stay…"

There had been talk of block-booking trains, planes and buses for the momentous occasion, but they settled for a carriage on the early train to Dublin. The man himself had travelled up the previous day and spent the night in a city centre hotel preparing his maiden speech. In all, just over 20 of them boarded the train. They were later joined in Banteer by supporters of newly-elected Fianna Fáil TD for Cork North West, Michael Moynihan, who filled the next carriage.

The craic was mighty all the way and, as reporter Catherine Halloran observed, there were bemused smiles from passengers getting on and off the train at various stations. "There was no doubt about it, even up as far as Thurles, they all knew who Jackie Healy-Rae was and were curious to see if he was on board. All through the train journey, there was a huge presence of children wandering up and down the carriages with pieces of paper in hand. They were looking for autographs," she wrote in *The Kerryman*.

As the train reached Portlaoise, accordion music could be heard coming from the carriage occupied by the Moynihan entourage. Not to be outdone by a Fianna Fáil TD, Danny Healy-Rae also produced an accordion and belted out *The Rose of Tralee* and *The Wild Rover*. The noisy crew eventually arrived at Leinster House and, despite tabloid reports that Jackie had demanded

Danny Healy-Rae leading the celebrations on the train to Dublin.

100 passes as part of his deal with Bertie, only a select few were allowed in. They rest stayed outside and staged a sing-song on Kildare Street.

The media turned out in force and Jackie didn't disappoint. With a roguish glint in his eye, he told them he would 'open a few dykes and fill a few potholes' and work for the ordinary people of the constituency.

In the press corps was the indefatigable Liam Fay, of *Hot Press*. "As someone who interviewed the Kilgarvan kingmaker at some length, a couple of years back, I know that he is neither the stage-culchie nor the clown he may appear. Despite their protestations to the contrary, however, most Fianna Fáilers treat him as a bit of a joke. There was certainly plenty of smirking and winking going on from both TDs and their lickspittles."

Jackie was the centre of attention, grabbing the limelight from other newly-elected TDs and big-name, established politicians. RTE almost missed the arrival of Bertie Ahern and his two daughters because of the hullabaloo being kicked up by the Healy-Rae gang. Many TDs approached to shake his hand. "Well done, ya devil ya," was the greeting from Fine Gael's Alan Dukes.

The pensioner TD was also the object of some teenybopper hysteria or Jackiemania. About 60 girls on a school outing spotted him through the railings between Leinster House and the National Museum. They started chanting, "Jack-ie! Jack-ie! Jack-ie!". Some climbed on the railings to get a better view. "After about 20 minutes, during which the chant had grown raucous enough to crumble concrete, Jack-ie himself looked over and acknowledged his fans with one of his robust victory waves. They went apeshit! Their cries and yells suddenly swelled into a fully-fledged MGM song 'n' dance routine," reported Fay.

As 3pm approached, the hour at which formal proceedings in the Dáil chamber were due to commence, the Healy-Rae crowd repaired to nearby Buswell's Hotel to watch the action on a large monitor in the bar. It was like waiting for the throw-in at an All-Ireland final. Pints began to flow and silence fell as the clock ticked towards three.

There had been speculation about whether Jackie would wear his cap in the solemn portals of Leinster House. That was soon cleared up. As he entered 'that big house', he lifted the tartan and placed in his jacket pocket where it remained until he re-emerged from the Dáil later in the afternoon. He was well turned out in a smart navy suit, yellow shirt and red, spotted tie.

The welcome in the chamber was warm and his speech declaring his support for the new, Ahern-led government was eagerly awaited. It was easily the most colourful contribution of the day. When he rose to his feet, murmurs went around the chamber and packed public gallery in anticipation of what he might say. From the beginning, he made it clear he was there to represent the people of south Kerry, first and foremost. Roads, farming, extending the tourist season were among his priorities. He finished his speech with a 'don't write me off' warning.

By evening, the ballyhoo had died down, his supporters were on the train home and he was getting down to work. Healy-Rae had scarcely warmed his seat in the Dáil when he was being dubbed the Kingmaker from Kilgarvan.

Jackie outside the Dáil. (© macmonagle.com)

He was enjoying the kind of privileged position a backbench Fianna Fáil TD could never dream about. A good man to generate a laugh in others, he was now having the last laugh – at Fianna Fáil especially.

He was the leader of the Government-supporting Independents, who were given two key links to the Government. Main link was Government chief whip Seamus Brennan whom they met after Cabinet meetings, usually on Tuesdays. Brennan, who had been general secretary of Fianna Fáil for many years, was a brilliant political operator. His job was to keep them informed of Government decisions, to ensure they were kept onside, that they had access to Bertie and to ministers and were present for Dáil votes.

Declan Ingoldsby, a civil servant in the Taoiseach's department, was another link to Bertie and a trouble-shooter who helped iron out any knotty issues they had with Bertie and their agreements. Bertie wanted to keep them happy at all costs and the Independents worked as a team. Healy-Rae, for instance, helped Blaney secure funding for a bridge in Donegal after it looked he mightn't get it.

After a settling-in period, *The Irish Times* parliamentary correspondent Michael O'Regan, a Tralee man who had first observed Healy-Rae in action in Kerry County Council, a quarter of a century earlier, noted he was the

Jackie in relaxed pose in government buildings. (© macmonagle.com)

most astute of the Independents. "He has settled easily into the Dáil, sitting on the Independent benches with Donegal's Harry Blaney and Wicklow's Mildred Fox, as well as the Dublin Independent TD, Tony Gregory, and Lispole's Joe Higgins, Socialist party TD for Dublin West. He is the chairman of the Environment Committee and has an open door to the Taoiseach and ministers. In the aftermath of the by-elections, these doors will open even wider."

'The tail wagging the dog' soon became the most hackneyed cliché when there was talk about Healy-Rae and the power he and the other Independents wielded over the Government – to the great annoyance of Fianna Fáil backbenchers. Fact was the Independents had much more muscle than the party's TDs when it came to getting things done in their constituencies. In November 1998, Fianna Fáil TD for Carlow-Kilkenny Liam Aylward said there was no point in being a Fianna Fáil backbencher any more. "Jackie Healy-Rae is running the show. He's running Fianna Fáil. It's kind of obvious. That's the way it seems," he protested.

Healy-Rae had succeeded in getting the Government to add Kerry and Clare to the list of areas that would qualify for Objective One, or maximum EU funding. He forced the Government to reclassify Kerry as disadvantaged so that it could stay on the EU gravy train. Only 13 counties had previously been included. What he had succeeded in doing fitted in neatly with his campaign for more cash for areas like south Kerry and he took full political credit. "I took the coat off and went to work on it," he said.

"Why should Kerry and Clare be included? Who conceded that?," asked Aylward, pointing out that the south east of his constituency was at least as deserving as either of those counties. He had raised the inclusion of areas in his own constituency many times at party meetings and had yet to receive an explanation as to why they were excluded. It was a terrible blow to every Fianna Fáil backbencher if Jackie Healy-Rae could get his own county included, he moaned.

The EU mandarins, however, did not accept the reasons put forward by Ireland for including additional areas for Eurostat funding and turned down the Government's submission. There was scathing criticism of the Government in the media, with the line being the whole submission was revised to ensure Healy-Rae's continuing support.

"There's little doubt that the Government is now paying for the public perception that it capitulated to political extortion by Jackie Healy-Rae," wrote *Irish Examiner* columnist Ryle Dwyer. "It was not that Jackie did not have a good case, but that the Government mishandled the whole thing from the start by initially announcing that only 13 counties would be included in the Objective One area. When Kerry and Clare were later added, no real effort was made to justify the change on legitimate grounds... Eurostat resented the appearance that our Government was asking the EU to pay what looked like a political ransom on behalf of the minority coalition in Dublin."

In early 1999, Healy-Rae was in the news for threatening to withdraw his support for the Government if it went ahead with plans to impose rates on bed and breakfast houses. Again, this was an issue that mattered in south Kerry, a leading tourist area. For once, Healy-Rae said he didn't want to be the tail wagging the dog, but he would be talking seriously to

Jackie could cause revolt

POWER: Healy Rae

Independents upset ordinary deputies

JACKIE Healy Rae could provoke a revolt among backbench TDs in Fianna Fail.

Ordinary deputies are getting cheesed off at the power wielded by the few Independents propping up the Government.

And Bertie's attempts to reassure them is cutting no ice.

"There is no point in being a Fianna Fail backbencher anymore," protested Fianna Fail TD for Carlow-Kilkenny Liam Aylward.

Running

"Jackie Healy-Rae is running the show. He is running Fianna Fail. It's kind of obvious. That's the way it seems," added Aylward.

And Waterford FF Deputy Brendan Kennelly said backbenchers were being treated like "lobby fodder".

After Healy-Rae claiming credit for getting Kerry into the area for maximum EU funding, it's hard to argue with Hyland.

Carlow has at least as good a case to make, but it doesn't have an Independent TD propping up the Government.

Junior Minister Willie O'Dea is annoyed too at Limerick being left out, as is Limerick West TD Michael Collins.

Dangerous

There's nothing as dangerous as disgruntled TDs in your party, though the euphoria of this weekend's Ard Fheis will help deflate some of the anger.

Bertie will have another problem too, if the Government's decision to add Clare and Kerry to the poorer 13 counties, backfires in Brussels.

If the EU throw out Ireland's bid, then Bertie will have egg on his face.

> "I went at it with my coat off." — Jackie Healy Rae on how he persuaded the Government to win Kerry's battle for more EU funds.

> "What about the disadvantaged areas of south-west and north-west Cork which are adjoining Kerry?" — Deputy P J Sheehan.

> "We don't have Jackie Healy Rae to speak for us." — Senator Therese Ridge (FG).

> "The Government is playing Russian roulette with the rail service. Irish Rail has 92 derailments and 18 collisions each year." Ivan Yates (FG).

How *The Star* newspaper read the situation on November 21, 1998.

the Government. They were talking about small B&Bs where it was the woman of the house that did most of the work herself and such businesses should not have to pay rates, he argued.

Healy-Rae had a formidable ally in Tourism Minister Dr Jim McDaid, who, given that he was from Donegal, was also strongly opposed to the plan as were others in the Government. The unpopular plan was dropped and Healy-Rae's vocal opposition to it did him no harm with voters back home.

In November 1999, came positive news, with Tanaiste and Enterprise Minister Mary Harney announcing a 300-job operation to replace the Pretty Polly company, in Killarney. The multi-national Sara Lee Corporation was to move into the former Pretty Polly factory, which had employed more than 1,000 people manufacturing ladies' tights at its peak, in the 1970's.

The replacement of Pretty Polly, in Killarney, was part of Healy-Rae's deal with Bertie and he was fast out of the traps to claims the kudos. Justice Minister John O'Donoghue claimed he, too, had played a critical role in getting Sara Lee to locate in Killarney, saying it was a joint lobbying effort. Healy-Rae was often first to announce good news for the constituency, much to the chagrin of O'Donoghue who claimed he had worked equally hard to get projects and grants for the area. This cat and mouse game between the pair continued for many years.

Sara Lee was enthusiastically welcomed in Killarney, an area which largely depended on tourism but which was short of jobs in manufacturing industry. Unfortunately, Sara Lee eventually closed in Killarney some years ago and the sprawling Pretty Polly plant stands idle.

Relations between the Independents and Ahern were good and there appeared to be no risks to the Government's stability. From time to time, the Independents looked for clarification on various issues and had to apply pressure when they felt that was necessary. Healy-Rae regularly made it clear that he would continue to vote with the Government as long as it honoured its commitments to him.

There were no signs any of the Independents would bring down the Government. Healy-Rae, Blaney and Fox were all in the Fianna Fáil blood grouping and that was the primary reason the party wanted to do business with them from the start. Tony Gregory, the Dublin Independent who was now outside the fold, believed the Independents had sold themselves short to Bertie. (His own deal with Charlie Haughey had never been fully implemented).

Gregory believed they should have demanded to be represented at Cabinet. If, for instance, the decision to seek Kerry's inclusion in Objective One region had been part of a collective Cabinet decision, and not seen as a political stroke, it would have a better chance of being accepted by Eurostat, he pointed out. Looking ahead, Gregory offered advice to the increasing numbers of Independents who were going be elected in future years: "If governments are going to be put together with the help of very small parties, then Independents will realise that unless you are at Cabinet table you will always be chasing after ministers and you will have much less effect."

In April 2000, Healy-Rae was getting exercised about a something close to his heart – the pub trade. While he stopped short of threatening to pull down the Government, he wanted to talk to Ahern about new proposals by Justice Minister John O'Donoghue. Healy-Rae said the proposals in the Intoxicating Liquor Bill 2000 were a disaster and criticised the failure of the bill to extend Sunday night opening beyond 11pm. He also disagreed with a proposal to shut down pubs that served alcohol to minors.

In short, Healy-Rae wanted pubs to remain open until 1am all year, with last drinks served at midnight. At the time, the Independents were carrying out a mid-term review of their support for the Government and co-ordinating their demands on a number of issues.

O'Donoghue, reared in a pub in Caherciveen, was adamant that the Bill, which would also abolish the two-hour closing on Sunday afternoons, would not be changed. He had consulted widely with the drinks industry, Gardaí, parents and other groups and was satisfied he had read the public mood correctly.

Healy-Rae stressed he was not in favour of under-age of drinking, but the closure of pubs caught serving under-18s was simply not on as it could ruin people's businesses. "Jesus man, that wouldn't be done in Russia," he remarked. O'Donoghue moved on regardless. Most of what he wished for became law and pubs still closed at 11 o'clock on Sunday nights.

The Independents met Ahern and told him they wanted opening hours seven nights a week to be extended, but he told them he could not do that because he wanted a country where people would get up for work on a Monday morning! The Independents had a meeting with John O'Donoghue who told them the Government needed the four votes to pass the Bill, so they withdrew and had a meeting among themselves. They decided to support the Bill, knowing the electorate would not thank them for causing a government to fall over demands to keep pubs open later. For once, the Independents didn't get their way.

As a publican himself, Jackie had a few prosecutions for late opening.

On one memorable occasion, he tried to get customers out of his premises by having the national anthem played a second time. But the crowd was so big the ploy didn't work and the Gardaí eventually arrived.

———————•———————

In the year 2000, he also did his own mid-term review of progress with his deal for Kerry South. He was aware the electorate would judge him on that and Fianna Fáil would be all out to win the seat back from him. There was no hiding the rivalry between himself and John O'Donoghue, but he conceded they also worked together and O'Donoghue had done things for him. He also joked he was one of the four wheels under O'Donoghue's state Mercedes.

At constituency level, there was relentless competition between himself and O'Donoghue for political credits. Sometimes, he would be first with news announced on Radio Kerry or in the local papers. "Jackie used to drive John O'Donoghue around the bend and John would go ballistic at times," Ahern recalled, years later.

Listing his achievements in 2000, Healy-Rae mentioned Sara Lee, in Killarney, and work on a series of roads, including the road to Kilgarvan, from the Cork side. Around £400,000 had been spent on the road. He continued to press for a new pier in Cromane for which the funding was approved. However, the pier has not built to up to 2015, with local disagreement on its proposed location and other issues locally being delaying factors.

Also among his achievements, he listed grants for other piers and harbours, funding for sewerage schemes and inclusion of farmers in a state fodder scheme. He also worked to prevent the sale of the state-owned Great Southern Hotels, two of which were in his constituency, but the hotels were sold to private interests some years later. His was not unqualified support and there were times when Fianna Fáil seemed to think it still had an overall majority, he observed.

In 2000, he issued warnings of civil disorder as a result of a flow of refugees and asylum seekers into the country, putting the number at a wildly exaggerated 80,000. Reflecting the public mood in some areas, he said resentment was building up and he was receiving the height of abuse from people over why he was not pulling the plug on the Government. A few weeks prior to that, his son Michael claimed the majority of asylum seekers were 'free loaders, blackguards and hoodlums'. Jackie backed him, saying he had to have good reason to say that and his son's supermarket in Kilgarvan was being targeted by some of these people.

Human and civil rights groups were incensed. And there was predictable media reaction. Writing in *The Sunday Tribune*, Stephen Collins said, since being elected, Jackie Healy-Rae had been treated indulgently as something of a national character, but the joke was beginning to wear thin. "Most recently, his dire warnings of civil disorder as a result of the refugee crisis have further inflamed an already delicate situation and sent ripples through the political system." Collins said there were less than 16,000 refugees in the country and Healy-Rae hadn't the slightest intention of pulling the plug on the Government.

Healy-Rae later clarified his position, saying he welcomed people genuinely fleeing persecution, but believed not all were genuine and feared the impact they might have on the country. It was a situation the Government was struggling to manage. People in some towns and rural communities had raised concerns about how they could cope with a sudden influx of people from faraway lands and vastly different cultures. But, despite some negative and over-the-top reaction around the country, things did eventually settle.

———————— • ————————

It was ironic that Jackie Healy-Rae was doing most of his talking outside the Dáil. He rarely spoke in the august chamber. In contrast, John O'Donoghue said more there than anybody else. Three years in the Dáil and very little said! Would that harm him in the next general election? Not a chance. As he'd say himself, he wasn't sent up to Dublin to be shouting in 'that big house'. Years later, he would say he did nearly all of his shouting at the Tuesday meetings with Seamus Brennan. His voters wanted him to deliver to them and the constituency and it was usually on Tuesdays the real business was done, behind closed doors.

There was, however, plenty of bluster from him during his Dáil career, especially when controversial votes had to be taken involving budgets and spending cuts. He often gave interviews on the plinth, but Bertie Ahern never doubted his support and he never voted against the Government.

Many years later, after he had retired, Bertie recalled how he would discuss issues in a reasonable way with Healy-Rae and he never took any notice when he heard him on the Morning Ireland programme, or some other media, the following day making all kinds of threats. "It was all a game," admitted Ahern, who added that once Healy-Rae was kept satisfied about local issues, the Government was guaranteed his support.

Healy-Rae would rail about something the Government was doing and would then go in and vote for it. It was in his interest to keep the Government in office for, if it collapsed, his deal would also go up in smoke. Bertie's retrospective comments didn't please Healy-Rae family members, who felt he seemed to have taken their father's support for granted.

During his first term in the Dáil, the economy began to improve and it was his most successful term in relation to getting things done. His focus was strictly on Kerry and whenever he spoke in the chamber, it was about issues relevant to the constituency. He could be seen talking to ministers and had a particularly friendly relationship with Agriculture Minister Joe Walsh, a TD for neighbouring West Cork. He had a reputation as a hard worker, coming in early and going home late. Though friendly, he breakfasted alone in a corner of the canteen and his demeanour was generally business-like.

In 2001, as an election neared, he was well established as an Independent and was making it abundantly clear that he would never return to Fianna Fáil. If he did that, he could lose some of his non-Fianna Fáil votes.

After four years in Leinster House, he warily approached the next election, knowing it would be a battle. In Dublin, he still looked every inch a countryman when among 'the suits' and city folk, while still keeping in close touch with the grassroots at home. He hadn't taken a holiday since being elected and had hardly a minute to himself, he let the world know.

6

Clinging to the Seat – 2002 Election

As he faced into the 2002 general election, uppermost in Jackie Healy-Rae's mind was the fact Fianna Fáil would be trying to win back what it regarded as its seat. But his trump card was he could tell the people he had delivered for the constituency through his deal with Bertie Ahern.

Having surprisingly topped the poll in the 1997 election, he also had to guard against complacency - his opponents were saying he was a 'certainty' to be re-elected. Healy-Rae had been around long enough to know otherwise and had to put out the message it was not going to be easy.

A hard-fought election it turned out to be. As they trod the roads and housing estates in search of votes, the Healy-Rae foot soldiers again wore out shoe leather. It was a workman-like campaign, even if it lacked the raw energy and sense of fun that were there for Healy-Rae, five years before. No discos this time and no rush of youth behind the ageing candidate. No longer a novelty.

The so-called sympathy factor had also dissipated and every vote had to be won on merit. The only 'certainty' for a seat was John O'Donoghue whose profile was at its peak: the two other seats were up for grabs.

O'Donoghue was elected comfortably on exceeding the quota. Moynihan Cronin got home on the sixth count and Healy-Rae had to wait until after the seventh count before being declared elected. Tension between the Healy-Rae and Fianna Fáil camp was palpable at the count centre, in Killarney. As he battled for his political life, Healy-Rae must have felt like a condemned

GENERAL ELECTION, MAY 15, 2002, KERRY SOUTH, FIRST COUNT (QUOTA: 9,162)

O'Donoghue, John (FF), 9,445
Fleming, Tom (FF), 6,912
Healy-Rae, Jackie (Ind), 6,229
Moynihan Cronin, Breeda (Labour), 5,307
Fitzgerald, Seamus (FG), 4,539
Casey, Sheila (FG), 1,934
Grady, Donal (Ind), 1,346
Barry, Donal (Ind), 934

RESULT: O'Donoghue (over quota), Moynihan Cronin (6th count), Healy-Rae (7th count).

man in the colosseum that was the count centre that day.

The temperature and tensions rose even further when Fianna Fáil sought a recheck after its second candidate, Tom Fleming, trailed Healy-Rae by 203 votes at the end of the seventh count. The recount made no difference to the result, though it put fire under Healy-Rae who blamed Fianna Fáil, and not Fleming, for seeking it.

"I was absolutely shocked," he stated, unable to hide his bitter feelings. "After keeping them in government for four or five years that they'd stoop so low this evening. But I wasn't one bit surprised and the longer it went on, the more confident I was of being elected."

He had dropped 1,000 votes since the previous election and it was a close call, but Fianna Fáil blew a chance to take out Healy-Rae and there were recriminations, internally, about the party's vote management. Fianna Fáil had enough votes to take two seats. Problem was, however, that O'Donoghue was too strong and more should have been done to split the votes more evenly between himself and Fleming. An old Fianna Fáil supporter was heard to describe their candidates as being 'like two horses

Jackie Healy-Rae has words of consolation for political rival Tom Fleming,
Fianna Fáil, after Mr Fleming's defeat in the 2002 Election.
(© macmonagle.com)

pulling a plough in opposite directions'. The result fuelled resentment in
the Fleming camp - something that would come back to haunt Fianna Fáil
in Kerry in the future.

With the country enjoying the Celtic Tiger era, both Fianna Fáil and the
PDs won extra seats nationally. Fianna Fáil now had 81 and the PDs eight.
The numbers enabled them to form a government - with Bertie as Taoiseach
and John O'Donoghue as Minister for Arts, Sport and Tourism - that didn't
require anything like the same level of support from Independents, 14 of
whom were elected.

In July 2003, nevertheless, Ahern confirmed a member of his staff was
maintaining regular contact with the Independent deputies who had kept
the previous Fianna Fáil/PD minority government in power for its full
term. The civil servant was assisting the Government chief whip's office in
liaising with the Independents, Healy-Rae, Mildred Fox and Niall Blaney,

Donegal North-East, who replaced his father, Harry, in 2002 election.

The official met the Independents on a regular basis and arranged to keep them briefed on issues as they arose. Ahern made it clear their support was not as critical as formerly to his Government's majority. But, he still wanted to keep them on board and would 'continue to try to be as helpful as possible' to them.

Fine Gael leader Enda Kenny complained the arrangement made a mockery of the equality of elected representatives to represent the people, as the Government was giving specific and direct support to named individual deputies. He also claimed officials from the Department of the Taoiseach were dispatched to Kerry on various occasions, not just to consult Deputy Healy-Rae, but also his son, and to walk the beaches and the roads while discussing events in general.

"I understand he offered advice to the Taoiseach in a threatening manner and said that he should have his bicycle chain oiled up at all times," Kenny added wryly. "Does that not represent an insurance policy paid for by the taxpayer in the event of the Taoiseach having an unhappy relationship with the Progressive Democrats?"

Ahern replied there had been regular contact between the Government chief whip and the Independents in the previous Dáil for good reasons because of the numerical issue. "That is not the case now," he explained. "The contact is not as frequent. However, these and other deputies look for assistance on different matters and we always try to deal with them. Government decisions are not made on that basis."

Obviously, the Independents did not have the same clout as formerly, but Bertie still needed to keep them sweet in the event of a PD pull-out, or some unforeseen mishap that could threaten his majority.

Healy-Rae attended in Leinster House from Tuesday to Thursday each week, spending most of his time on constituency matters. He would lunch quietly in the members' bar each day, and not on spuds beloved of people who have their dinner in the middle of day – he preferred soup and a lean beef sandwich! After a weekend at home meeting constituents, he would bring back an amount of work which he would try to have dealt with before the end of the week. While in Dublin, he would phone the bar in Kilgarvan each night, usually around closing time or later, to find out how things were going. The family dubbed it, Call from the Dáil.

During weekends at home, he spent time on the farm at Rae. In 2006, there was a brief diversion from political hurly-burly when one of the animals, his pet pony called Peg, was stolen from the farm. For a change, it was the pony, not himself, that made headlines. He discovered she was missing on an evening after returning from the Dáil, proclaiming himself 'broken-hearted' and offering a EURO 1,000 reward.

The Gardaí made inquiries and Peg was found some weeks later, near Newcastlewest, Co Limerick, in a fairly dishevelled state and tied to a gate. It looked as if she had been used a workhorse, but he soon pampered her back to the condition to which she had been accustomed, feeding her with crushed oats.

Jackie Healy-Rae with close friends, Maurice Galvin and Dermot O'Callaghan. (© macmonagle.com)

Healy-Rae always treated health issues as a priority and made it his business to understand patients' needs and how best to deal with them. He was chairman of the old Southern Health Board and made many useful professional contacts while in that role. Working from the bottom up, he knew who to contact and where to go. He developed a reputation as a man who could get things done in the health area - finding a hospital bed for somebody, getting an appointment or a medical card and numerous other representations.

Many tributes were paid to him following his death in December 2014, but there was some surprise when one appeared in the *Irish Medical Times*, the weekly newspaper for doctors. In an appreciation, Dr Gary Stack, of Killarney, recalled how his relationship with Healy-Rae went back to the time he and a colleague, Dr Donal Coffey, were trying to establish the SouthDoc out of hours GP service in Kerry. They approached all local politicians. Two weeks later, they got a phone call from the office of Health Minister Micheál Martin telling them seed money was being forwarded to get the project off the ground.

"We knew nothing further about how this came about until Micheál (Martin) himself stated in his speech at the official opening of SouthDoc that it was Jackie who had forced his hand. We found out that Jackie had gone to two other co-ops already operating in the country to find out what these co-ops were about," wrote Dr Stack.

A cheque had been written for an extension to an existing co-op and all that had to be done was to change the name on the cheque. Curiously, Dr Stack noted Healy-Rae had never said anything to him, or other local doctors, about that and had never claimed the political credit for it.

However, Healy-Rae was not slow in claiming credit for helping thwart plans by the Department of Health to close district hospitals in Killarney, Kenmare, Caherciveen and parts of west Cork. Later, there were rows with other Kerry politicians over credits for securing new community hospitals for Dingle and Kenmare.

As a TD, Healy-Rae continued to attract media attention. In July, 2006, Kevin Cullen, of the *Boston Globe*, accompanied him to Glencar Cattle Show & Carnival, in the shadows of The MacGillycuddy's Reeks

"When Charles J Haughey, the silky voiced, elegantly attired, and perpetually embattled former prime minister of Ireland, died last month, many pundits suggested that an era of colorful *(sic)* politics went into the ground with him," Cullen reported. "Those pundits obviously don't get out of Dublin much, and they certainly don't come down to County Kerry in Ireland's southwest, where Jackie Healy-Rae is proof-positive that the colorful *(sic)* Irish politician is not extinct. At 75, Jackie is the oldest member of the Dáil, Ireland's parliament. He is also its greatest character."

He also related some of the apocryphal stories that have passed into folklore. Like the suggestion that gondolas be put on the lakes of Killarney to attract more tourism, to which Healy-Rae is reputed to have replied:``Sure, but who would feed them?" Another was the occasion when his mobile phone rang and he demanded of the caller, ``How'd you know I was here?"

Cullen noted that Jackie was the first to admit he was part of a dying breed. "As Ireland's economic fortunes have risen, so have politicians' view of themselves. The Dáil, to which Jackie was first elected in 1997, used to be a place that didn't take itself so seriously, he says.`The boys up there now think they walk on water,' Jackie says, waving a hand dismissively. Jackie is well-loved in Kerry because he reflects so many of its people and traditions. He has been a farmer, a publican, a mechanic, a musician, a sportsman, and a contractor."

Irish Independent columnist Kevin Myers, however, took an entirely different line, arguing that Jackie's populist image camouflaged a less wholesome reality, an era of backroom politics that some say died along with Haughey.

"Jackie Healy-Rae personifies the world of the secret deal, the hand slapped on the stairway, the meeting for the purpose of a free and frank exchange of opinions, at which everything is decided well in advance," Myers observed. Continuing in that vein, he compared Healy-Rae to a sketch, a circus show and a likely subject for a Punch cartoonist, with the famous headgear last seen on an Irish scalp in the film, *The Quiet Man*.

Healy-Rae's constituents take little notice of such remarks from people 'above in Dublin' who don't understand their ways. Constituents saw him as a character, not a caricature, and obviously thought he represented them well by electing him and members of his family on numerous occasions. Cullen quoted observers in Kerry as saying that while some people in Dublin saw him as something of a buffoon, that was a gross injustice. In Kerry, he was respected as a self-made man, someone who had to take a lot of responsibility when he was very young.

The American journalist also accepted that even Myers, a withering critic, acknowledged that politics in Kerry is all about the delivery of services and that Jackie delivered. He was one of the politicians credited with getting Government money to keep Kerry roads so smooth that, as Myers said, 'you could iron silk knickers on them.'

— 7 —

The 2007 Election and a Tough Third Term in the Dáil

As the 2007 general election approached, Healy-Rae asked himself if it was time to step down. After consultations with the family and his inner circle, the 76-year-old decided to stand for the last time. Again, it proved to be a testing election for him and there was a further drop in his vote. The veteran came into the campaign wide open to attacks from political rivals after supporting the Government's controversial cuts to health services, in particular. To add sizzle to the heat in the pan, the economy was also on the slide; the good times were over and worse, much worse, was to come.

At a pre-election rally in Killarney, scenes reminiscent of by-elections in the 1960's and '70's were witnessed. Lines of men carrying pikes topped with blazing sods of turf marched through the streets led by Jackie Healy-Rae, who was flanked by family members and key supporters. Hundreds of people took part in the spectacle which, the Healy-Raes later said, was important to their success in the election. A picture of the parade by Killarney photographer Don MacMonagle received widespread publicity and framed copies can be seen in bars, hotels and other places of public resort.

On the night before the election, a phone call made to a man, named only as Joe, by a persuasive Michael Healy-Rae, reflected serious worry, even signs of desperation, in the camp. When Joe said he was giving his number one vote to another candidate, Michael offered 'to go down on my knees' before him seeking a number one for Jackie.

Michael's line was that John O'Donoghue would be the first to be elected and Breeda Moynihan Cronin, Labour, the second, but his father would be fighting for the third seat. The phone call, which gave an insight into Healy-Rae canvassing skills, later went viral. As the election turned out, Moynihan Cronin lost her seat and Healy-Rae survived.

GENERAL ELECTION, MAY 24, 2007, KERRY SOUTH, FIRST COUNT (QUOTA: 9,759)

O'Donoghue, John (FF), 9,128
Fleming, Tom (FF), 6,740
Healy-Rae, Jackie (Ind), 5,993
Sheahan, Tom (FG), 5,600
Moynihan Cronin, Breeda (Labour), 5,263
Fitzgerald, Seamus (FG), 4,195
Ni Bhaoigheallain, Lynn (SF), 1,375
Hickey, John (Green Party)

RESULT: O'Donoghue (3rd count), Sheahan (5th count), Healy-Rae (6th count).

Healy-Rae did better on transfers from Moynihan Cronin, who lost her seat to Sheahan, and managed to stay ahead of Fleming to take the last seat.

It was another close one for the Kilgarvan man who obtained 15.35 per cent of the vote, compared with 17 per cent, in 2002, and 20.34 per cent, in 1997. If the decline continued, the seat would be in real danger come the next election. As in 2002, Fianna Fáil took only one seat and, again, there were post-mortems in the party on its vote management which allowed Healy-Rae hold on to his seat.

Nationally, Fianna Fáil won 78 seats, down three, and the PDs two, down four. The Green Party won six seats and agreed to form a coalition government with Fianna Fáil and the PDs. The three parties had a six-seat majority, with Ahern as Taoiseach. Ahern made separate agreements with Healy-Rae and Tipperary North Independent Michael Lowry in return for

FIANNA FÁIL
THE REPUBLICAN PARTY

Agreement Between Bertie Ahern TD, Uachtarán Fhianna Fáil and Jackie Healy-Rae TD

The following sets out the basis of agreement between us, which will cover the full term of the 30th Dáil.

I will endeavour to ensure that all of the commitments listed in the programme of priorities below will, to the best of my ability, be acted upon.

In return I am seeking your vote for my election as Taoiseach and your continuing support for the Government during the full duration of the 30th Dáil.

Access to members of Government

I am happy to arrange reasonable access to me, as Taoiseach, in the event that serious difficulties arise in connection with the delivery of the programme. Similarly, I will arrange for you to have contact with the relevant Ministers when issues arise within particular portfolios that are of interest to you.

In normal circumstances, however, I will designate a person in the Taoiseach's Office who act as your contact point for day to day matters as they arise.

Dáil Time

I will ensure that Dáil time is provided for you out of the Government allocation to enable you to address issues of importance to you and your constituents in the Chamber.

Government Announcements

I will ensure that you have adequate foreknowledge of the announcement of proposals that are of particular interest to you or your constituents. In this context, I will also ensure that matters of general interest to you or to your constituency will be made known to you at the same time as other Government Ministers.

An agreed Programme of Priorities

The following are certain matters that we have agreed should be set out as priorities.

There may be difficulties from time to time on certain projects and we will endeavour to expedite them.

My main priority is to implement the National Development Plan with its massive €184 billion investment as a hugely important further step in transforming Ireland and ensuring a better quality of life for all our people.

The priorities are:

- To sustain and grow employment all over Ireland but particularly in the county of Kerry as it has experienced job losses in the last while.

- Sustainable jobs must be created in Killarney, Kenmare and Kilgarvan. Accessibility to indigenous industries to be allowed into IDA held facilities.

- Making Broadband accessible for all in County Kerry where possible and using alternative mechanisms such as landline and mobile/wireless services in areas of particular difficulty such as the Black Valley, Inny Valley and Lauragh.

- Community Development Funding to be allocated to South Kerry for community supports.

- Review the National Lottery applications for qualifying projects in south Kerry.

- Implementing the legislation to change the name of Daingean to Dingle Daingean Ui Chuis.

- Funds to be made available to restore Killarney House to add to the attractions for tourism, which employs thousands of people in Kerry.

- St Finian's Land use should be clarified and proposals from the St Finian's Community Group should be taken on board if at all possible.

- Implementing Transport 21 in full so that the infrastructure in Kerry will be made accessible and attractive for business creation.

This will include:

- Relief road for Kenmare. 2 years with a viewing to earliest possible start date. (€5m)

- L3013 from Killarney to Gneeveguilla 20kms will be improved within 3 yrs. (€8m)

- Road improvements to the N70 from Scariff Inn to Caherdaniel within 3 years. (€3.5m)

- Foleys Bridge on the N70 will be renovated during 2008. (€300,000)

- A roundabout at the joining of the N22 and N72 (Lissivigeen) commencing 2007 (€500,000)

- A new bridge at Barraduff with new road alignments going into it from both sides to commence 2008. (€4m)

- N71/N22 link (Castlelough to Lissivigeen) over a 4 year period. (€18m)

- The bridge at the N70 at Curraheen will also get attention during the lifetime of this Government. (€4m)

- Funding for the L4040 for the 2.6km from Gap Cross to Tomies Cross.

- Removal of turns on the L3003 within 3 years. (€350,000)

- N22 needs a right hand lane within 2 years. (€250,000)

- A roundabout at Shinnagh Cross for safety reasons within 2.5 yrs. (€500,000)

- L2033 needs to be continued from the Park Cross to D. O'Sullivans at Doneen. (€1.7m)

- L32021 needs to be upgraded from Morley's Bridge to Incheeses within 2 years. (€150,000)

- Junction XT88 needs to be automated.

- Improvements to the non-national bridges in the Kenmare engineering area to ensure safety (€1.5m)

- Improvement works to the L4074 (€1m)

- N71 – design and construction of improvements at Farrell's bend (€350,000)

- Kilgarvan to Poulgorm R569 within 2 yrs. (€2.5m)

- Killarney area non-national bridge improvements (6 bridges) within 3 years. (€1.5m)

- Improvement works on the L7060 Local Secondary Road. (€1m)

- Road from Lissivigeen to Barraduff. (€2m)

- N72 road from Barraduff to Rathmore (€5m)

- Blackwater Bridge to Sneem village over 3 years (€7m)

- Gaddagh Bridge – finish works (€0.5m)

- R571 – Improvements (€2m)

HEALTH

- Access to breast screening for the women of Kerry by 2008.

- Construction of Dingle Hospital to commence.

- Extension to Kenmare Hospital to be commenced. Day Care Centre also to be built which will include services for the mentally ill.

- Cystic Fibrosis facilities to be upgraded at CUH.

- Provision of a sexual assault unit in Kerry General Hospital.

- Review the Carers Allowance.

- Assess the need for an MRI scanner for Kerry General with a view to providing funding for same.

- Upgrade the existing orthodontic dental service in Kerry.

- Provide funding for a public playground in Kenmare and other towns to allow children to exercise.

EDUCATION

- 4,000 new primary teachers to be provided to meet demographic demands and reduce class sizes.

- Enable children with Autism to benefit from a range of teaching approaches, including ABA, PECS and TEACCH, as appropriate.

- No reintroduction of 3rd level fees.

Signed

Bertie Ahern TD
Uachtarán Fhíanna Fáil

Jackie Healy-Rae TD

(**AUTHOR'S NOTE:** This agreement was declared 'confidential' at the time it was signed, shortly after the 2007 election, and the copy was obtained from sources independent of Fianna Fáil and the Healy-Rae organisation. As the document was signed by Mr Ahern as President (Uachtarán) of Fianna Fáil, it cannot be obtained under the Freedom of Information Act.)

their support. Initially, they were joined by Dublin Independent Finian McGrath, who withdrew his support over a year later due to health cuts. By now, austerity was becoming a dreaded byword and it was cuts all the way because of the dire economic situation.

In a post-election speech from the back of a lorry, in Kenmare, Jackie Healy-Rae bore all the signs of a man who had come through a bruising battle. He had come under pressure from his old party for the seat he had retained for a decade. Like Michael's phone call, his speech also made it to YouTube. MC Niall O'Callaghan announced, 'sugar daddy is back' and the crowd chanted in reply, 'siúcra, siúcra, siúcra'.

Alluding to his councillor sons, Danny and Michael, Jackie told the crowd that because they had voted for him, they had three people working for them. "You've got good value for your vote you gave me yesterday – three for the price of one… Many's the house I went to in the west who said,'of course you'll get our vote. If it wasn't for Michael Healy-Rae, we wouldn't have planning permission for this house, this turn wouldn't be taken or the potholes wouldn't be filled.' I got that message all over the place."

Michael also got in on the act, working up the crowd by telling them that nobody would ever 'bate' the Raes.

Back in Leinster House, a short time later, the Healy-Raes were conferred with an unexpected political advantage, which they exploited to the full. On June 14, 2007, John O'Donoghue was elected Ceann Comhairle, or speaker, of the Dáil. The office of speaker has to be seen to be neutral and 'above politics' and it limited O'Donoghue in what he could do in the constituency in the way of attending events, claiming political credits, or turning up at party functions. As the new Dáil assembled on its first day, Jackie Healy-Rae caused amusement when he rose to congratulate the robed O'Donoghue.

"I congratulate the Ceann Comhairle in a very special way. I congratulate him because I go back to when I directed elections for him in the early years. God knows, I played a leading role in sending him to this House in the first instance," he declared, to laughter around the chamber. A chuckling Ahern and his finance minister, Brian Cowen, were barely able to contain themselves.

"I wish him many long and happy years in the seat in which he is now sitting. Standing here this evening, I guarantee the Ceann Comhairle that if there's a bad pothole around Waterville, on Dursey Island, in west county Cork, or anywhere in Caherciveen, I will do my very best…in the Ceann Comhairle's absence, I will do my best to sort them out and I will keep him well informed all the time."

There was a brief reply from O'Donoghue: "I assure the deputy that I will never be far away." The clip of the televised proceedings is still shown occasionally on television.

On April 2, 2008, Bertie Ahern announced his resignation as Taoiseach and Brian Cowen was formally elected to replace him at a parliamentary party meeting on April 9, becoming Taoiseach on May 7. In a letter to Healy-Rae, dated April 30, Cowen confirmed he would honour Ahern's agreement.

A few months later, speculation that his family's local political organisation would amalgamate with Fianna Fáil before the next general election was firmly dismissed by Michael Healy-Rae. This followed an announcement from Jackie that he would not contest that election. The timing of the announcement was perceived as a clever move to give Michael, the heir apparent, plenty of time to consolidate his base.

"I do not see the two organisations merging soon or in the long-term," Michael stated. "We have run an independent organisation since my father first won the Dáil seat, in 1997, and that's the way I think it will stay."

Comparisons were being made between Kerry South and Donegal North-East, where the Independent Blaney organisation returned to the Fianna Fáil fold, in July 2006. The reconciliation brought an end to a bitter, 35-year rift and Niall Blaney became a Fianna Fáil TD for the constituency.

Some of the speculation regarding a similar reconciliation in Kerry arose from a deal made on Kerry County Council involving Fianna Fáil, the Healy-Rae brothers and Sinn Féin. It secured the prestigious mayoral post for Michael Healy-Rae. Since the 1997 break from Fianna Fáil, however, the Healy-Raes have been consistently emphatic they would never consider returning to the party.

LETTER FROM BRIAN COWEN TD TO JACKIE HEALY-RAE TD

Mr Jackie Healy Rae TD,
Dáil Éireann,
Leinster House

30th April, 2008

Dear Jackie

Further to our meeting today, I want to thank you for your good wishes on my taking up the office of Taoiseach next week and for your continuing support for the Government.

I wish to confirm that the basis for your continued support for the Government is the political agreement signed by you with the outgoing Taoiseach and President of Fianna Fáil, Mr Bertie Ahern TD. I look forward to working with you in that regard.

I also wish to confirm that it is my intention to liaise with you during the course of this administration to ensure that progress is made on the implementation of that agreement and I will do everything in my power to fulfil the agreement in the context of our administration running its full term.

Yours sincerely,

Brian Cowen TD
Leader-designate, Fianna Fáil

———————————•———————————

In October 2008, meanwhile, Jackie Healy-Rae did not rule out dropping his support for the Government because of education cutbacks. He was concerned about the growing pupil-teacher ratio in south Kerry schools. The Government was coming under pressure from all sides to row back some of its heavy budget cutbacks. Healy-Rae addressed the nation on RTÉ radio's Morning Ireland programme, but didn't withdraw his support. The heat was also coming on him arising from controversies over medical card cuts and in areas such as farming. But he still hung on.

In August, 2009, he threatened to vote against the Government over cuts to the rural transport programme. His comments were dismissed as 'bluster' by Fine Gael, which was mindful of the fact that he had backed Fianna Fáil since he was first elected, in 1997, and had a special deal with the Government in three, Fianna Fáil-dominated administrations.

Crucially, his support and that of Lowry was becoming increasingly important as the coalition's Dáil majority dwindled. In times of plenty, such a situation should give the Independents' muscle to wring further concessions for their constituencies, but now the opposite was the case.

By mid-2009, Healy-Rae and Lowry conceded cuts would have to be made to their deals because of the economic climate. Healy-Rae was being realistic. For example, his 2007 agreement included EURO 4m to replace one of Kerry's most notorious bridges, at Barraduff, on the Killarney to Mallow road. But, at a meeting with then Transport Minister, Noel Dempsey, he agreed to the existing bridge being widened and the road realigned at a considerably lesser cost of just €1.5m.

In October 2010, the long-awaited Castleisland bypass was officially opened. Costing €35 million, it was the only new road building scheme to be started by the National Roads Authority in 2009. As might be expected, credit for the bypass getting through an embargo on new schemes was claimed by Healy-Rae. He had used his position as a Government supporter to 'at all times put the interest of the people (of Kerry) first,' he declared.

Danny, Jackie and Michael Healy-Rae at Castleisland bypass official opening.
(© macmonagle.com)

He chided the Opposition for criticising his advantage and told them to stop trying to jeopardise items he had agreements on.

He turned up for the bypass opening with his councillor sons, Danny and Michael. Photographers snapped the trio together, with the pictures appearing in the following day's papers. "Look coming, it's the triple bypass," quipped one wag on seeing the Healy-Raes arrive.

All the while the economic situation was worsening. In November 2010, the Government sought an International Monetary Fund (IMF) bailout, with the EU and international agencies also involved. At the height of the crisis, Jackie Healy-Rae stepped from a taxi outside Leinster House where he was met by a bustling media corps including international television crews. Asked if he would continue to support the coalition, he looked confused and replied:"I don't know what's going on…I'm just up from the bogs of Kerry."

It was as if the emergency rocking the country had nothing to do with him. The clip of his answer made the news programmes that evening. But, the situation was becoming more difficult for the Independents and the Government started to fall apart towards the end of 2010.

In January 2011, Healy-Rae and Lowry, who got on well together, warned their support for the Finance Bill was not guaranteed. But, the Government had to find a way to get the Bill - the law needed to implement the Budget - passed quickly. After meeting with Taoiseach Brian Cowen and, separately, with Finance Minister Brian Lenihan, to resolve some issues, both voted for the Bill which was passed. The crisis-ridden Government's days – and Healy-Rae's tenure in Dáil Éireann - were coming to an end, however.

A vote of confidence was passed in Cowen by the parliamentary party, but was opposed by Foreign Affairs Minister Michael Martin and other prominent Fianna Fáil TDs. There were resignations and Cowen announced he was stepping down as Fianna Fáil leader, on January 22, but continued as Taoiseach until a new government was formed after an election, on February 25, 2011. Following Cowen's resignation, the Greens also confirmed they would be pulling out of government.

It took until 2012 for details of Bertie Ahern's 2007 'secret' deal with Healy-Rae to become public on RTE. The deal included projected spending of almost €66 million on 26 Kerry roads over five years. But, due to the abrupt ending of the Government and the economic crisis, not all of the package was delivered. Building work on Kenmare Hospital, only six miles from Kilgarvan, was also listed as a priority in the Healy-Rae agreement.

Lowry's deal had more than a dozen pledges on health, including the development of a surgery centre of excellence, at Nenagh Hospital. School buildings, care centres for the elderly and a public swimming pool in Roscrea were also among the more than 40 local priorities set out in the agreement. His agreement also dealt with road improvements.

The deals guaranteed the Independents access to the taoiseach and his ministers. They were told about matters that concerned them at the same time as Government ministers and TDs. Again this caused problems for Fianna Fáil TDs, especially when Healy-Rae and Lowry outflanked them by being first with announcements of 'goodies' for their constituencies and thereby claiming the credit. Usually, the FF TDs would also have lobbied on the same issues.

A senior civil servant in the taoiseach's office was the Independents' contact point on a Dáily basis and they were promised speaking time in the Dáil. Not everyone was happy with the agreements, with former Government chief whip Tom Kitt describing parts of the deals done with the Independents as unsavoury.

Despite coming under attack from groups such as widows, social welfare recipients and organisations like the Kerry Public Service Workers' Alliance (KPSWA) for his support for the deeply unpopular Government, Healy-Rae stood his ground until early 2011 when it went out of office.

The criticism hurt most when it came from Kerry. The following is an example of the hard-hitting language used:"In one of the most nauseatingly opportunist of political moves, Fianna Fáil supporting TD Jackie Healy-Rae has finally said he may not support the Government anymore…Can this be the same person who less than a year ago refused to say whether he would support the Government in future cuts, who claimed that he had no power?," a KPSWA statement said.

"Healy-Rae's propping-up of the hugely unpopular government is only one of a long list of reasons why the Healy-Rae dynasty should be in for a nasty shock come the next election," the statement thundered on.

Confirming he would run for his father's seat at the next election, Michael Healy-Rae said voters wouldn't hold Jackie's support for the Fianna Fáil/Green Government - the most unpopular in Irish history - against him. He read it correctly - the voters of Kerry South duly elected him. The message from his voters was that delivery on local issues was more important than the welfare of an ill-governed country that was broke, being bailed out and at the mercy of strangers.

In March 2012, *The Week In Politics* programme, on RTE, revealed details of the 'confidential' 2007 deals with Healy-Rae and Lowry. At the start, presenter Sean O'Rourke referred to 'pork barrel politics' – a term which is American in origin and which basically means the spending of government money in a constituency to gain support for a local politician.

Getting away from it all with American country star Charley Pride at the INEC, Killarney. (© macmonagle.com)

Setting the tone of the programme, O'Rourke asked if local issues should be allowed dictate national decisions on how money was spent over two Dáil terms, and how individuals used their influence to secure pet projects for their constituencies.

Senior Fianna Fáil figures regularly insisted any spending in the Independents' constituencies was part of the programme for government and was money that would be spent anyway. But, only the most politically-naïve believed that. Everyone knew the deals were outside the programme. Up to the end, the straitened Government could find money somewhere to satisfy the Independents - illustrated by Healy-Rae's squeezing of at least €1m out of Brian Lenihan for road works locally, as the Government was in its death throes.

Healy-Rae's 2007 deal had a detailed section on road improvements. An extension to Kenmare Hospital was also pledged. A new hospital opened in Kenmare, in June 2013, and the Healy-Raes angrily locked horns with local Fianna Fáil Senator Mark Daly over the political credit for delivering the project.

Several of the demands were met, especially in relation to road projects, including sections of the Ring of Kerry; others were not. Construction of Dingle Hospital was completed, but a sexual assault treatment unit has not been provided in Kerry General Hospital. In national terms, many of the projects were small and localised, but important to the people. For example, a new roundabout at Lissivigeen, on the main Killarney to Cork road, and the widening of the bridge at Barraduff were important for the easing of traffic problems locally.

Parts of the three-page deal were aspirational and non-specific, including the creation of jobs, in Kerry, providing broadband and improving landline and mobile phone services, for instance.

Correspondence between Cowen and Healy-Rae showed the deputy's concerns about putting 'nappies', or dung catchers, on jarveys' horses, in Killarney. Not all requests were granted – a call to appoint former Kerry footballer Pat Spillane to the Sports Council went unheeded. While not written down in formal deals with Fianna Fáil, it does appear Healy-Rae and Lowry secured up to six places on state boards for people they knew.

At the end of the programme, *The Week In Politics* reporter Micheál Lehane noted critics would always regard such deals as damaging to the national interest and they would be described as examples of pork barrel politics. "But, with 15 Independents elected last year (2011)," he added, "many people, it seems, are more than willing to cast their votes in the hope that their local TDs might just become very powerful when the government is formed."

In relation to the 2007 deal, Ahern and Cowen signed themselves, Uachtaran Fhianna Fail and leader-designate Fianna Fáil, respectively, which meant the details could be not be accessed under the Freedom of Information Act. Though funded from the public purse, the agreements in 1997 and 2007 were both declared confidential when signed, which gave rise to concerns and provided ammunition for the Opposition.

Jackie Healy-Rae was almost 80 when he retired prior to the 2011 general election. Advancing years and the relentless march of time had caught up with him. Those close to him had noticed how he had tired during his last term in the Dáil which, due to an ongoing series of cutbacks and resultant pressures, he found extremely difficult.

Despite the rumpus he kicked up about Bertie Ahern ignoring him prior to the 1997 election, he developed a good relationship with the three-time Taoiseach of Fianna Fáil-led coalitions. He seemed to have liked Ahern, saying there were 'no tricks or blackguardry' in him and he was honourable to deal with. As for Cowen, Healy-Rae felt the Offaly man was 'not as articulate' as Ahern and didn't have his finger on the button as much.

Whenever Ahern went to seek his support for a new government, Jackie would present him with a list of demands for the constituency. "The list would be as long as your arm but, most of the time, I'd cave in to his demands," Ahern admitted. The former taoiseach also stated, much later, that deals with Healy-Rae amounted to a 'pittance' in terms of the national finances and the money had been well spent on necessary projects.

In retirement, Healy-Rae enjoyed rural life and more time on the farm at Rae with his animals, including his pony, a donkey and three dogs. He would travel from Killarney to Kilgarvan each day, arriving into the family bar at around 11am. There, he would check the mail and have a cup of tea with son Danny's wife, Eileen. Then, it was up to the farm where he fed the animals and might get to work on a machine. He once said he liked nothing better than meeting a man smelling of grease – a reflection of his love of all kinds of machinery.

Keeping an eye on what his sons and grandson were doing, he still took an interest in politics. As he and many people in Kerry South saw it, he was fortunate to be in a position to negotiate deals for the spending of money in the constituency during his 14 years in the Dáil.

Fianna Fáil, however, argue that John O'Donoghue - especially when he was Minister for Arts, Sports and Tourism - brought more investment and funding into Kerry than Healy-Rae. O'Donoghue, for example, was able to use National Lottery money to deliver grants to a large number of sporting organisations, in Kerry, for building and upgrading their facilities. Following his defeat in the 2011 election, O'Donoghue pointed to the irony of the count taking place in a public sports centre, in Killarney, which could not have been provided without funding secured by him.

Claims for credits by various politicians and political parties continue. But, Kerry would probably have had to wait for much longer for many projects which were expedited because Healy-Rae could extract deals from governments in return for his support.

There's no doubt he secured tens of millions of euro for the constituency, chiefly for spending in road projects. The fact that his entire focus was unapologetically local led to criticism from some sources in Dublin, who liked to disparage him as a parish pump politician and worse.

Critics disagreed with his demanding of favours for his constituency on the grounds that only national issues should be considered in the national parliament. But could not every TD of the 166 be described as a parish pump politician to a significant degree? After all, they have to be elected and must, therefore, take care of constituency issues to garner their votes. Ministers also deliver as much as they can for their constituencies, as John O'Donoghue, and Dick Spring before him, did for Kerry.

In 1982, newly-elected Independent TD Tony Gregory wasn't the subject of the same level of fury as Healy-Rae when he pulled off a deal for Dublin's north inner city in return for his support for a minority Fianna Fáil government led by Charlie Haughey.

While nobody could dispute the claims of Gregory's long-neglected, urban heartland for special funding, a similar argument could also be made for Kerry South, a largely rural constituency with its own problems of unemployment, isolation, depopulation and a lack of investment in transport and other essential services. Healy-Rae's stomping ground was no different to many other areas in the west of Ireland.

During his second and third terms in the Dáil, he sometimes found himself in a dilemma. Problem was he could only get favours for the constituency by continuing to support the Government. If he withdrew that support, whatever agreements he had would also go. So, he had to put up with the criticism that came his way to ensure the terms of his agreements were honoured as far as possible and, of course, to ensure the voters sent another Healy-Rae to Leinster House.

As Healy-Rae saw it, his role very simply was to represent the people who elected him and be an advocate of their needs and wants. Towards the end of his life, he was asked if he would do anything differently. "No," he replied, without a second's hesitation, "but I'd try to do a hell of a lot more of the same."

Fine Gael Senator Paul Coghlan, from Killarney, seemed to develop a close relationship with Healy-Rae and they often travelled to Dublin together. It was a relationship that was forged, in the 1990's, when both were members of Kerry County Council. While Coghlan enjoyed the older man's company, seeing him as a jovial, charismatic character, he also regarded him as an able politician.

"He was a very effective leader of the group of Independents that supported Bertie Ahern as Taoiseach from 1997 to 2002," Coghlan recalled. "He knew what he wanted and how to get it. He knew who to ring and who to go to. His agreements did deliver - no doubt about that."

———————— • ————————

Deal-making with Independents has helped create political dynasties and looks like continuing to be part of future governance in Ireland. Regardless of the national interest, pragmatism rules. The experience thus far has been that if major parties, or coalitions of parties, are a few votes short of forming a government they will do deals with Independents to attain power.

The trend in recent elections has been to elect an increasing number of Independents. Aside from disillusionment among the public with political parties, part of the reason for the popularity of Independents could be that voters see an advantage in having an Independent in their constituency, given the experience of Healy-Rae, Lowry and others in winning concessions for their constituencies.

Healy-Rae enjoyed a long political career, spanning five decades since he was co-opted to Kerry County Council, in 1973. First and foremost, he was a constituency politician, with the emphasis on the local, which continues to be the Healy-Rae priority. He set the template and laid the foundations for the successful Healy-Rae political and business dynasties that look like being around for a long time.

Like many other families, emigration was part of life for the 'Raes'. Most of his siblings emigrated and, during his retirement, some people tried to persuade him to visit them in America, but he didn't do so. He never liked flying and was happiest pottering about the farm.

His siblings in the US first went to their uncle, Mike Healy, in New York, and he helped them settle there. Denny, Hannie and Kathy, emigrated in the early 1960's. Mick went to England before going to New York in the mid-1960's. Jackie's step-brother, Timmy, is living in Walsall, England. Most of Jackie's surviving siblings are in New Jersey. Mick and Denny drove buses in New York and were there when another Kilgarvan man, Mike Quill, brought the city to a standstill as leader of a Transport Workers' Union strike, in January 1966.

Jackie and partner Kathleen Cahill. (© macmonagle.com)

Quill died suddenly of a heart attack, three days after speaking at a mass rally to celebrate a new contract for his members, from which the Healy brothers also benefited. He was involved in the War of Independence and took the republican side in the Civil War. Quill was an uncle of former senator and Progressive Democrats TD Mairín Quill, who was also born in Kilgarvan and who lives in Cork. The old Church of Ireland church, in Kilgarvan, is now the Michael Quill Centre.

Kathleen Cahill

For decades, Kathleen Cahill, Jackie Healy-Rae's partner and secretary, was the woman in the office, taking the phone calls and answering queries from constituents. She was the person that put some order into the often chaotic life of a busy politician who was rushing here, there and everywhere, keeping appointments and being at the public's beck and call. She became an indispensable part of his life and he once described her as 'very, very excellent'. Some newspapers couldn't resist calling her 'Jackie's rae of sunshine'.

In December 1974, Kathleen, from Kilcummin, outside Killarney, was widowed after her husband, John Cahill, died in a car crash near Cork city. Aged twenty-three at the time, she was left with a six-month-old daughter, Antoinette. John, also from Co Kerry, had worked in construction in Chicago. Kathleen, a psychiatric nurse, had visited the Windy City and they were planning to return there when tragedy struck.

She first encountered Jackie when she went to him about a political matter some time after John's death. Later, they met socially. Though from a Fianna Fáil-supporting family, Kathleen had little interest in politics and had never voted. Jackie was the first person she voted for. She didn't work after John's death as she was rearing Antoinette at their home, in Killarney. But, she gradually started to help Jackie with his county council work.

After his clinics, he would come to her with his notebooks on which requests from voters had been handwritten in big letters. She would then type out letters to various departments and officials, making representations on behalf of the people who had come to the clinics. She also maintained a filing system.

Occasionally, there would be some impossible requests from clients. "I'll certainly try, but I don't know if you'll get it," he might tell them. Having tried, Jackie would always come back to them, whether the result was good or bad. "While he was always glad to be able to do something for people, he also believed in telling them if he couldn't deliver," she said.

With some trepidation, she kept an eye on Kerry's progress in the All-Ireland football championship each year. For, if Kerry reached the final, there would be requests for tickets. As there was no point in looking for tickets in Kerry, that meant a string of phone calls to TDS, senators and councillors in other parts of the country. Jackie, who would meet people on match mornings outside the Gresham Hotel, in O'Connell Street, usually came up with the tickets.

Election times were hectic. She recalled a Healy-Rae supporter, Seamus O'Connor, driving her around in his Mercedes with a loud speaker on top of the car, festooned with posters during campaigns in the 1980's. She sat in the back seat with a recorder and, in each town they went to, she would play the song, Rise and follow Charlie. "It shook the towns and villages and the animals were flying around the fields. It was such fun and then Seamus would ask for their number one vote for Charlie," she said.

At the time, Jackie was director of elections and he regularly delivered two seats for Fianna Fáil in the constituency. The party's election office was in Donie O'Shea's, High Street, Killarney.

Jackie loved Christmas, one of his rare periods of relaxation, and they had the same routine each year, she recalled. After dinner on Christmas Day, they would put on Bing Crosby tapes and any other Christmas videos they would have been given him as presents. It was much the same on New Year's Eve. At midnight, he would count one, two, three and fire two shots up into the air. Her brother, Thomas, would fire them as well across the fields. A bottle of champagne would always be opened. Sometimes, friends Donie and Noreen O'Sullivan came over and Kathleen's brother, Liam, was always in the company. Jackie would phone his family and brothers and sisters, in New Jersey, to wish them a Happy New Year

All that was an enjoyable break from Jackie's political life. During his election campaigns, phones never stopped ringing and canvassers were in

Jackie with Antoinette Cahill.

constant contact. Dealing with calls and constituents' problems had an added urgency and Kathleen's life was on a 24/7 carousel. On 'normal' days and nights, Jackie was forever on his mobile phone, but needed several phones during an election. He also made Dáily visits to the farm in Kilgarvan to which he had been committed throughout his life.

Sometimes, politics and social life mixed for Jackie and Kathleen. They would meet friends in Scott's Hotel, Murphy's Bar and the Failte Hotel, in Killarney, and in Collins' Bar, in Kilcummin. A light drinker, Jackie enjoyed a nip of Canadian Club whiskey. He never went anywhere without his notebook and biro and always gave time to a constituent, no matter where he found himself.

Jackie was also devoted to Antoinette with whom he had a warm relationship. In Kathleen's words, he was 'mad about Antoinette' who currently works as social catering director, managing weddings and other functions at The Drake Hotel, in Chicago. Equally, he was close to Antoinette's daughter Katie, now ten.

Kathleen – the woman responsible for the tartan cap – also looked after Jackie's style. She would go with him to buy his clothes and would arrange for Antoinette to bring matching shirts and ties on her trips home from the US.

When she first met Jackie, he wore a black Cossack, or Astrakhan, hat, which she did not like. Something smarter and more colourful would be just the thing and more in keeping with his ebullient personality, she thought. So she got some flat, tartan caps in Quill's fashion store, in Killarney. The caps became an instant hit. Following Jackie's election to the Dáil, in 1997, there was huge demand for the caps. Many were given away as presents, for charity auctions and spot prizes at social functions. Jackie also presented one to Gay Byrne during a *Late Late Show* appearance.

Now that he was in the Dáil, Kathleen's workload also increased enormously. He never bothered to get the hang of a computer, but she began using a computer for all of her secretarial work. Jackie was a stickler for punctuality and always aimed to get to places before the appointed time, if at all possible.

In July 1999, Jackie shared the front page of *VIP* celebrity magazine with Bertie Ahern's then partner, glamorous Celia Larkin. But the story wasn't about himself; it was about the special woman in his life. "Her name is Kathleen Cahill and she's an excellent girl," he declared. "She's unequalled for constituency work and she's very, very excellent.'

He told how she became his secretary when he was elected to the Dáil two years previously. She had been working in a government department and he had the option of choosing the people he wanted to work with, he pointed out. After his election, he immediately looked to have Kathleen appointed. Her job wasn't easy, he conceded. "You've no idea how tough! There are three phones hopping around her all the time. It's an extremely difficult job, to put it mildly, but you could get nobody as good as her."

The admiration was mutual. "He was very committed to doing what he could for people and had boundless energy. He never seemed to get tired," Kathleen said. "Sometimes, he'd get upset about something and there might a 'few words' with somebody, but he'd move on from that and didn't keep up a grudge. His greatest satisfaction was in helping people. I miss him terribly. He stood out in the crowd and you'd always know he was around. There'd be no fun without him".

Whenever he had a quiet hour, he liked nothing better than to relax before a blazing turf fire listening to music, country especially. His morning read was the *Irish Examiner* and he always returned later in the day with the *Evening Herald*.

While he enjoyed generally good health in the early years of retirement, he had put on weight and slowed a little. He was also troubled by one of his knees for which he underwent surgery and his health began to deteriorate in the first half of 2014. Almost a year after his death, Kathleen finds it hard to believe he's gone. "I feel he could still walk in the door," she said.

———————— • ————————

8

The Changing of the Guard – 2011 Election

The 2011 general election brought huge changes nationally and in Kerry, which failed to return a Fianna Fáil deputy for the first time ever. Fianna Fáil received a massive drubbing from an angry electorate growing tired of austerity, down from 78 to 20 seats. Fine Gael and Labour were given a resounding mandate to form a new Government, with a total of 113 seats.

In Kerry South, three new deputies were elected. Michael Healy-Rae succeeded his father as an Independent; former Ceann Comhairle and senior minister John O'Donoghue lost his seat as did Tom Sheahan, of Fine Gael. It was third time lucky for another Independent, former Fianna Fáil general election candidate and councillor, Tom Fleming, who had been narrowly defeated in two previous elections, while the youthful Brendan Griffin took over the Fine Gael mantle from Sheahan. A boundary change, which saw a population of 5,098 around Castleisland and Cordal transferred to the constituency, benefited Fleming as he hailed from that general area.

Despite all the fire his father came under for supporting such an unpopular government, Michael Healy-Rae managed to hold the 15 per cent share of the votes garnered by Jackie, in 2007. John O'Donoghue was the sole Fianna Fáil candidate, but his fortunes had faded dramatically since the 2007 election as he had lost his ministry and had become a reluctant Ceann Comhairle. Then, in 2009, he resigned as Ceann Comhairle in the wake of an expenses controversy.

The election is also remembered for the eloquent speech by O'Donoghue,

GENERAL ELECTION, FEBRUARY 25, 2011, KERRY SOUTH, FIRST COUNT (QUOTA: 11,096)

Griffin, Brendan (FG), 8,808
Healy-Rae, Michael (Ind), 6,670
Fleming, Tom (Ind), 6,416
O'Donoghue, John (FF), 5,917
Sheahan, Tom (FG), 5,674
Gleeson, Michael (SKIA), 4,939
Moloney, Marie (Labour), 4,926
Comerford, Oonagh (Green Party), 401
Behal, Richard (Ind), 348
Finn, Dermot (Ind), 281

RESULT: Griffin (5th count), Fleming and Healy-Rae (6th count).

at the end of the count, which had taken place in a sports complex which would not have been there but for funding provided through him. The election also marked the beginning of the end of the O'Donoghue dynasty, which started when John's father, Dan, was elected to Kerry County Council, in 1960.

While the Healy-Raes continued to be a dominant force in Kerry politics, the situation in Leinster House was no longer in their favour. With an abundant majority, Fine Gael leader Enda Kenny formed a coalition with Labour, which did not need the support of any Independents. At a time of big governing majorities, there was no way of trading a Dáil vote for 'goodies' for a constituency. However, Michael Healy-Rae soon became involved in Dáil business, putting down far more questions and speaking in more debates than his father. In 2012, for example, he spoke in 115 debates and received answers to 803 written questions.

That was an above-average performance, according to the Kildare Street. com website. In September 2015, the website reported he spoke in 114 Dáil debates and committee discussions, and received 1,058 answers to written questions, in the past year. The questions concerned issues such as medical cards, grants for farming and fishing, as well as health and social welfare services in general.

Down the years, Michael had been closely linked to his father. They worked together politically and were often photographed and appeared at public events together. Also, he was elected on much the same range of local issues as his father had been in three previous elections, all of which Michael directed. Though he has many of his father's traits and also wears a flat cap, dark as distinct from tartan, he set out to be his own man and to build a profile in the Dáil.

But, Jackie hadn't really gone away. In June, 2011, details emerged of correspondence in which he accused Brian Cowen of being motivated by 'self-preservation to the detriment of the Irish people'. On November 22, 2010, after the then coalition announced the intervention of the EU and the International Monetary Fund (IMF), the deputy threatened to withdraw his support for the Government, by now nearing the end of its days in office.

In a faxed letter to Cowen, released under the Freedom of Information Act to the RTÉ programme *The Week in Politics*, Jackie Healy-Rae wrote: "Not alone did the Taoiseach of this country tell blatant lies to the Irish people regarding the IMF and the ECB, but his cabinet ministers to a man were singing from the same sheet."

Although, he urged Cowen to call an election and 'stop this charade of spin and lies,' Healy-Rae did not follow through on his threat and continued to support the embattled coalition, like many times before.

The day after the Dáil was dissolved, in February 2011, Healy-Rae wrote another letter to Cowen. He said he was expecting to hear from the Taoiseach, in the days ahead in relation to the R569 road to Kenmare and the eastern Kenmare bypass. "I want this money ring-fenced for these two projects," he demanded.

In June 2010, Mr Cowen wrote to Mr Healy-Rae to confirm his son, Michael, would be appointed to the National Treatment Purchase Fund's board. "Following our recent discussions on the matter, I now wish to confirm that I have spoken to my colleague Ms Mary Harney, who has agreed to appoint Cllr Michael Healy-Rae to the board," he wrote. However, Michael Healy-Rae was not appointed to the board.

The honeymoon period for Healy-Rae Junior in the Dáil was short. If he hadn't known already, he soon learned morning sunshine doesn't last all day. Unlike his father who had been in favour with previous Fianna Fáil-led governments, the new coalition had no intention of obliging the Healy-Raes. In July 2011, there was proof of that when Minister for Social Protection Joan Burton removed Michael Healy-Rae from his €6,000 per year post on the board of the Citizens Information Board.

Ms Burton wrote to him saying he was being dismissed because of a conflict of interest between his membership of the Dáil and his membership of a body advising the minister. She said the conflict arose because as a member of the board he could advise the minister but would then be able to vote on that advice in the Oireachtas.

After he refused to resign, she threatened to dismiss him. Healy-Rae, who had been appointed at the behest of his father, in April 2009, was due to remain on the board until 2014. He strongly disagreed there was a conflict of interest.

Around Leinster House, the rookie TD developed a reputation as hard worker, who focussed mainly on constituency matters while always keeping an eye on national issues of relevance to the constituency.

The House does not normally open until 7.30am each day, but he soon discovered a service entrance from Merrion Street opens at around 6.40am and began to use that. The idea is to get in early so as clear work from his desk before the phones start ringing, with so many other things to do later. For the same reason, he often works late at night.

He's also a regular on radio and TV programmes. As a family, the Healy-Raes have often been described as 'natural' media performers. In November 2013, they enjoyed a big publicity blast through a TV3 documentary, entitled *At Home with the Healy-Raes*.

Seen by hundreds of thousands of people nationally, the programme contained a mix of good and bad. Reporter Ciara Doherty, who seemed to be more exhausted than the Healy-Raes for her efforts, told how she had to be up before 6am to keep pace with Michael, who often didn't finish his day's work until after 11 o'clock at night. The impression of a frenetic lifestyle came across.

At the outset, Jackie compared the family to Santa Claus, as they appeared to be everywhere. But, Ms Doherty asked, at what price to the country as a whole? Jackie remembered the deal he cut for local road funding with then Finance Minister Brian Lenihan, in late 2010, in order to continue to prop up perhaps the worst and most unpopular administration in the history of the State.

"We went into Lenihan and he said, 'Jackie, we'll sort out your side of it today, What will it have to be?,' he said. In one word I said, 'it'll have to be one million,' I said. Lenihan gave me the million; there was no problem in the world." (It transpired later the sum was much higher). The programme inferred Jackie had helped keep them in power for a long time after they had clearly lost control of events, but that did no harm to brand Healy-Rae in subsequent elections.

Michael has described the Fine Gael/Labour coalition is one of the most anti-rural governments since the foundation of the State, accusing it of facilitating the demise of rural Ireland in many ways, especially by closing post offices.

———•———

In April 2015, Taoiseach Enda Kenny and his close advisers were heavily criticised by members of Fine Gael over their 'wooing' of Michael Healy-Rae and other Independent TDs, Michael Lowry, Noel Grealish and Denis Naughten, about supporting the next government, in advance of a general election.

Fast out of the traps was Kerry Fine Gael TD Brendan Griffin who said it was outrageous for the party to be considering doing business with people who had played a part in 'ruining' the country – a reference to the support of the Healy-Raes for three Fianna Fáil-led governments and to Lowry's for the previous government.

"Have we learned nothing? If we as a party were to do that, we would be going back to the bad old ways. It would be a sad day for the country,"

Michael Healy-Rae on the campaign trail. (© macmonagle.com)

Mr Griffin declared. He claimed such a deal would enable his constituency rival, Healy-Rae, to project himself as a kingmaker in order to increase his vote in Kerry.

Healy-Rae confirmed the approaches had been made, but he would wait until the election before making any decisions. As for Deputy Griffin, he asked: "What part of the money my father secured does he not agree with? What road would he not want built, what school would he not like there?"

In June 2015, Healy-Rae ruled out throwing in his lot with any of the new political parties, or alliances of Independents, saying he would not be joining 'any crowd in Dublin' but would be facing the people in the election as a true Independent.

Though an election has not been called at the time of writing, Healy-Rae has been canvassing and knocking on doors in the new Kerry constituency for several months. By early summer, thousands of canvassing cards had been printed. Brother Danny and nephew Johnny were listed as his directors of elections.

He is in uncharted territory in what was the former Kerry North/West

Limerick constituency, but has a significant plus factor going for him – instant recognition on the streets and doorsteps. No introductions needed.

The door-to-door canvass is being conducted in accordance with a proven modus operandi. The constituency chart is on an office wall, with names and phone numbers of supporters available for a canvass. The canvass works like this: always ensure a well-liked and respected local person is around to accompany the candidate; if you enter an estate or a village, don't leave until every house is canvassed; if a potential voter has a problem, take down details on the doorstep and deal with it as soon as possible. Don't knock on doors too late at night. At one time, Jackie Healy-Rae would finish a canvass before the 9pm TV news, but the family have been known to stretch that cut-off time a little, especially if in 'friendly' territory.

In comparison to his father, who specialised in church gate speeches, torch-lit parades and other traditional electioneering methods, Michael Healy-Rae is using more up-to-date ways of catching voters' attention. Outsize visuals and the social media, for instance.

As the next election, due in early 2016, approaches, anyone driving through Kilgarvan can't but be aware they are in Healy-Rae country. By September 2015, three, long truck trailers had been parked on the outskirts of the village, with huge posters of Michael Healy-Rae urging people to vote for 'experience and common sense' – the family's generic election slogan - while two other vehicles carrying the brand name are regularly parked in the village. Photographs of Danny and Johnny, which appeared on Carrantuohill during the 2014 local elections, are on display over the pub door.

9

The Local Politicians

If anyone epitomised the well-worn adage, 'all politics is local', it was Jackie Healy-Rae. It continues to be a guiding principle of his family. In retirement, he would say his happiest days in public life were the 30 years he spent on Kerry County Council. He loved being in close touch with the people and helping resolve their problems on the ground, literally.

Red tape and bureaucracy were often obstacles that needed to be got out of the way, or even ignored. There's a classic story of a pothole at the entrance to a housing estate in Killarney, which people swear is true. The pothole was getting deeper and deeper but, despite phone calls and requests to the local authority, no action was being taken to fill it.

Eventually, some bright spark decided to ring a certain man in a certain public house in Kilgarvan. The following morning, two men in a van arrived at the estate. Out they jumped, quickly producing a steel bucket of tar with steam rising from it. A few shovels of chips were then taken from the van, mixed with the tar and the pothole was filled, pronto. No fuss, or fanfare.

All this was done as people were heading to work and children were getting ready for school. Those that saw what was happening spread the word; soon, everybody knew, credits rolled in the Kilgarvan direction and they didn't forget who filled the pothole when the next election came. It wasn't the first time the Healy-Raes decided to take direct action to fix a problem.

Planning has always been a key political issue for the family going back to Jackie's earliest days on the council and his jousts with An Taisce. With their calls for an easing of planning restrictions, their approach to planning could be described as liberal. They believe strongly in allowing people build

Let 'em strip, demands Jackie

By DECLAN WHITE

KERRY'S County Council chairman has warned protesters to leave nudists alone.

Jackie Healy Rea blasted objectors to Ballybunion's bid to open Ireland's first bare-all beach.

Naturists with the heatwave are flocking to the Nun's Strand — beside a Catholic convent.

Skinny-dippers swim and glimpse dolphins off Ballybunion's secluded cove.

But a few vigilantes have been nagging tourists to keep their clothes on.

Now Council Chairman Jackie says protesters should "stay the hell out of there. There is no law or obligation for anyone to go to the nudist beach except people who want to. Other people don't have to go there."

"They are not asked, so it shouldn't upset them in the least and they should have no worry in the world about it."

Ballybunion has campaigned this sum-mer to open Ireland's first official clothing optional beach.

Local business people want to tap into Europe's naturist market numbering 30 million people.

A petition, to be presented at Kerry County Council's next meeting in September, has gained nearly 3,000 signatures.

And Chairman Jackie, from Kilgarvan, wants an open county council debate about

■ *Cllr. Healy Rea: "If people want to go without clothes why shouldn't they?"*

Ballybunion's nude beach.

"I see no reason in the world why we shouldn't try nudist beaches. I have no objections whatsoever.

"If people want to go without clothes why should they be made wear them? It's up to themselves in a secured beach in Ballybunion.

"We are not living in the grey old ages, for God almighty's sake. There is a massive market for this and that's why I have no objection to it.

"It's a modern world and we will have to keep up with the rest of them."

Cllr. Healy Rae's comments were welcomed last night by Ballybunion hotelier Frank Quilter, who said the council chairman, like himself, obviously saw the huge potential of naturism tourism.

He said there were 20 million naturists in Europe. They were high spenders and would boost tourism revenues.

Leave nudists alone, says Jackie Healy-Rae, *The Examiner*, 1996.

one-off houses on family-owned land. This sometimes brings them into conflict with fellow councillors and environmentalists, amid warnings from senior planning officials about damaging the scenic landscape of Kerry which is so important to the county's tourism industry.

Like many other counties along the western seaboard, the Kerry countryside is now peppered with one-off houses, sometimes obstructing views of mountain and sea which visitors come thousands of miles to see.

Former Fianna Fáil TD John O'Leary was one of those who disagreed with a lot of what Jackie Healy-Rae proposed in relation to one-off housing and relaxing planning restrictions. Prior to entering politics, O'Leary had been a planning official, an experience which taught him that planning permission needs to take account of the visual and physical environment.

As a councillor, Jackie also grabbed headlines for his views on other matters. Some people objected to people baring all on Kerry beaches in heatwave conditions during his second term as council chairman, in 1996. To make matters worse, there was a campaign to open a nudist beach in Ballybunion, amid reports naturists were flocking to the local Nun's Strand, near a convent of all places. But Jackie saw nothing wrong with it. "Stay the hell out o' there," he warned objectors.

There was no obligation on anyone to go to a nudist beach, except those that wished to do so and those people weren't harming anyone, he pointed out. Ballybunion still doesn't have such a beach, by the way.

He and son Michael worked together politically for many years and, it seemed, Michael would be expected to keep an eye on matters at county council level after Jackie's election to the Dáil, in 1997. One evening in 1998, the father and son were doing clinics in the Tuosist area when they picked up Joe Riney, a local supporter. Joe asked Michael if he was going to stand for the council. Taken aback a little, Michael replied he did not know.

Joe, however, helped him make up his mind when he more or less suggested he didn't have much choice, as Healy-Rae supporters in the Killorglin Electoral Area needed a Healy-Rae to vote for at council level. Jackie himself was, at this time, still a councillor for the Killarney area.

In 1999, Michael stood in the local elections and joined his father on the council, taking the fifth and last seat in the Killorglin area, following a close battle with Fine Gael's Johnny (Porridge) O'Connor. There was little between them and, at one stage, it looked as if O'Connor would take the seat on the grounds that a surplus from fellow Fine Gael candidate, Michael Connor-Scarteen, of Kenmare, would get him over the line. A few in Fine Gael had already begun premature celebrations.

Some in the Healy-Rae camp were inclined to throw in the towel, but Jackie hadn't given up hope. "This is not over yet," he cautioned. The old campaigner had been watching the count and had noted Scarteen's votes included a decent number of transfers for Michael. As Jackie had expected, people tended to vote for local candidates rather than on strict party lines. Kenmare is only six miles from Kilgarvan; the Healy-Raes are usually transfer-friendly and they got enough votes from Scarteen's surplus to take the seat.

Michael Healy-Rae, who lived outside the Killorglin Electoral Area

The last photograph of Jackie Healy-Rae. Taken on May 24, 2014, in Kerry General Hospital, he is keeping track of the progress of son Danny and grandson Johnny at the local elections count, in Killarney. (© macmonagle.com)

and, therefore, could not vote for himself, personally canvassed every house and business with the aid of a loyal band of supporters, many of whom had previously soldiered with his father. His plea to voters was to take a chance on him and to judge him on his performance. They could kick him out come the next election if he did not meet their expectations, he reminded them.

In 2003, Jackie Healy-Rae resigned his seat on the council for the Killarney Electoral Area because of the abolition of the dual mandate, which meant a person could not be a member of a local authority and the Oireachtas at the same time. He stepped out reluctantly. His view was that, as a TD, it was important to be in touch with the people at grassroots level so as to have a better understanding of issues. His son, Danny, was co-opted to the seat and that helped further tighten the family's grip on politics locally.

In the 2004 local elections, Michael doubled his vote in the Killorglin Electoral Area and added a further 1,200 votes in the subsequent election. He and Danny became the first set of brothers to sit side by side on the council since Pat and Timothy Connor-Scarteen, both Fine Gael, of Kenmare, were elected on the same day in 1955.

In 2007, Danny Healy-Rae, who regularly argues against planning refusals, was himself refused permission by An Bord Pleanála for a 38-house development near the main street in Kilgarvan. But he didn't appear too disappointed. Normally a fierce critic of constraints on development in Kerry, he reacted by saying he believed the appeals board may have done him a favour, as the housing market was on the slide at the time.

Earlier that year, Kerry County Council refused Healy-Rae's company, Gortnaboul Partnership, planning partly because of a deficiency in Kilgarvan's sewerage facilities. The council planners said the development would also be premature because a local area plan for the village had yet to be completed and he had not shown an urgent need for housing in the area.

Originally, he had planned to build 47 houses on the elevated site near his brother Michael's shop and petrol station, but had scaled the plans down with the council and prior to his appeal to An Bord Pleanála. He had envisaged a 'unique' sewerage treatment system that would not have impacted on the public system, but could be linked to it later, he pointed out. Even if he had got permission, he would not have proceeded for some time, given the poor state of the housing market, he said.

In May 2009, prior to the local elections, Danny Healy-Rae went public to fight off a dirty tricks campaign being waged against him and other members of the family. He took out advertisements in Kerry newspapers to respond to a 'vicious campaign', involving the circulation of anonymous letters, aimed at undermining his efforts to be re-elected.

Thousands of what was described as nasty, untrue letters detailing the earnings of the three politicians in the Healy-Rae family had been circulated, he said. "I don't engage in nasty politics. I am going before you on my track record and my ability to serve," stated the candidate in the Killarney Electoral Area in his newspaper notice.

He also chastised some political opponents for 'codding' the people by saying the long-awaited Castleisland bypass would not go ahead. Jackie Healy-Rae had claimed the credit for getting approval for the bypass.

In 2011, Michael Healy-Rae was elected to the Dáil and had to resign his council seat because of the dual mandate rule. Danny's son, Johnny, was co-opted to the seat and set about building up support for the next local elections, three years later, for which Michael would be director of elections. In the interim, Johnny had the benefit of political mentoring from his grandfather, father and uncle and was ready for road when the starting shot was fired for the 2014 elections.

Working on the basis that there's no substitute for meeting people face-to-face, Johnny got a turbo-fuelled campaign underway, out and about during the day, while reviewing and planning strategy with his team late into the night. Everyone knew Danny Healy-Rae would do exceptionally well in the elections and there was speculation about how many votes he would be over the quota. Johnny, however, was going before the electorate for the first time in the new South and West Kerry Electoral Area which took in much of the Iveragh and Dingle peninsulas.

Danny polled a gargantuan 4,388 first preferences, more than two quotas, and was a runaway poll-topper in the Killarney Electoral Area. He picked up 24 per cent of the vote, well up from close to 16 per cent in the previous election. Johnny also topped the poll in his area with 3,495 first preferences, 1,414 over the quota and 17 per cent of the vote. His uncle, Michael, had topped the poll in the previous election, but it was still an impressive showing from the newcomer. Johnny had mounted a typical Healy-Rae type campaign and had people of all parties and none working with him, including the likes of Fionan Hickey, of Kilgarvan, whose late father, Dermot, and Jackie Healy-Rae had been close friends.

Like an unstoppable political juggernaut careering through south Kerry, the father and son team amassed 7,883 votes, close to a quota in the old Kerry South Dáil constituency. Assuming that all were brand Healy-Rae votes, a big majority of them will be expected to go to Michael Healy-Rae in the next general election which would put him into a strong position as he faces into untested territory in the former Kerry North constituency, as Kerry will be just one, five-seat constituency.

Political talk after the 2014 local elections was that brand Healy-Rae could have got more candidates elected, given the size of the accumulated vote. But that didn't seem to bother them. The view in the camp was that if they stood other candidates, there was no guarantee the vote could be managed in the way they would have dictated. So, it looks as if a candidate has to have the Healy-Rae surname – to have others running for the organisation could dilute the brand and the dynasty.

Around the time of Jackie's death, the Healy-Raes got into a spat about the naming of a new road in Kenmare. It was a row between two local dynasties. The Healy-Raes wanted the inner relief road to be named after Jackie, but, in January 2015, the council voted overwhelmingly to dedicate it to the memory of ex-Fine Gael TD and county councillor Pat Connor-Scarteen, of Kenmare.

Johnny Healy-Rae said he had the highest regard for the Connor-Scarteen family, but asked that the people of Kenmare be consulted before a decision on naming the road was made, adding many people in the town told him they would like to have a say in the matter. However, the council rowed in behind the Scarteens, a respected Fine Gael family with a history dating to the Civil War. Like Johnny Healy-Rae, Pat Connor-Scarteen's grandson, Patrick Connor-Scarteen, is a third generation member of the council.

Posters on top of Carrantuohill prior to the 2014 local elections.
(© macmonagle.com)

While disappointed, Danny Healy-Rae said his father would be long remembered, even if a road in his own area was not dedicated to him. The Healy-Raes later declined to attend the official opening of the road. This affair happened at a particularly sensitive time and rankled the Healy-Raes who consistently and passionately defend their father's record.

Politicians generally tend to look on road projects as an important part of their legacies. They like to have roads, bridges or roundabouts named after them. In a situation mirroring what happened in Kenmare, Jackie Healy-Rae made it public he would have been honoured to have his name associated with a roundabout at Lissivigeen, just on the Cork side of Killarney. However, Kerry County Council decided to dedicate the roundabout to local woman Gillian O'Sullivan, a silver medallist in the world race walking championships.

Prior to the May 2014 local elections, some people scaled the heights of political gimmickry by placing elections posters with photographs of Danny and Johnny Healy-Rae on top of Carrantuohill, Ireland's highest mountain. A photograph of the posters received wide publicity, while some rivals cast their eyes skywards and questioned the legitimacy of the act.

The Healy-Raes said they themselves didn't go up the mountain. They didn't have time as they were too busy canvassing. "Some of our supporters did it and there's no truth in the rumour that my father went up there with his pet pony, Peg," said Danny, tongue-in-cheek. He promised, however, that the posters would be removed within the statutory, seven-day period after polling. A council spokesman said there was nothing against having posters on the mountain, as long as they were removed after the election.

It was apt that Jackie Healy-Rae should leave his sick bed in Tralee to go to Kilgarvan to vote for Johnny. On the day of the count, in Killarney, the young councillor also kept grandad briefed on what was happening, through mobile phone. And, characteristically, the ill patriarch wasn't hiding under the blankets when the kudos were being dished out. Speaking from his hospital bed, he attributed some of the big vote to the legacy of his own work as a TD.

As if the emphasise the priority the family attaches to local politics, Michael Healy-Rae is regularly at pains to stress his regard for councillors. A strong opponent of the abolition of town councils, which happened in 2014, he said one of the most hurtful things he had heard in the Dáil was a comment by the then Environment Minister Phil Hogan, who abolished the councils.

"When I said councillors were very upset, he got a fit of laughing and told me:'You can go back and tell them I'm quaking in my boots.' It was one of the most disgusting things I've heard in the Dáil and it showed total disrespect for councillors," he said.

⸺⸺⸺ • ⸺⸺⸺

The May meeting of Kerry County Council, in 2013, was well underway when a German TV crew, journalist in train, turned up at the council chambers, in Tralee. On the agenda was the filling of the seat left vacant on the resignation of Breeda Moynihan Cronin, a former TD and chairperson of the Labour party.

However, the German camera crew was focussed on Danny Healy Rae's campaign for a relaxation of drink driving laws and his call for special permits to allow rural drivers and others to have a few pints at the pub and then drive home. The campaign had found supporters all over rural Europe, the journalist with *Spiegel TV* said.

Long-time Kerry journalist and Rae-watcher Anne Lucey recorded the occasion like this: "Always approachable, 'they're following me,' Danny said nonchalantly, when I enquired. Germany was one thing, but the international calls had already come from Chile, Italy, Spain and France and, in fact, 'fore' (sounding like a golfer's warning) TV crews had so far arrived to interview him, from Germany alone, he said.

"The *Spiegel TV* reporter, Roman Lehberger, said Danny Healy-Rae's passion about rural matters was what impressed most. 'He acts as a counterweight to more densely populated areas, and through him, rural people feel they have a voice,' Mr Lehberger said.

"The rural passion is something which Danny's father Jackie, son Johnny and brother Michael all share and articulate. But an international, or even a national vision, is more accident than design.

"Pragmatic to the core, the Healy-Rae machine clears the briars to expose the local path rather than hack any new highway; there is always a receptive audience because the audience is hearing what it is thinking already and above all what it most desires is fed back with the rich Healy-Rae Hiberno-English rhetoric.

"This might be about loosening laws on septic tanks, or it might be Jackie questioning all the rubbish about recycling and advising the executive to go to the bog and dig the hole with the machine and bury it like he always had done. Or it might be the 'hunting' of families off the land and into towns rather than letting them build on their own land.

"These days, Michael is half-advising a relaxation of the gun licensing laws to allow rural dwellers to defend themselves against marauding burglars in a country free of Gardaí. But he is cute in the way he says it - he's not exactly telling them to get a gun either!

**Election celebrations for Michael Healy-Rae at a count in Killarney.
(© Valerie O'Sullivan)**

"If the Healy-Rae's have a rhetorical secret, it is the twin tool of exaggeration or understatement. However the devices are measured and rarely so outlandish as to be ridiculous – though sometimes they are and fall flat. 'You'd need good German to understand it,' Danny said of the German documentary on him.

"And when it came to the great, rolling controversy surrounding the rebuilding of the famine ship, the Jeanie Johnston, which threatened to break two Kerry local authorities and was actually stuck in a shed, at Blennerville, unable to move across the silted bay, county manager Martin Nolan informed the council he had cut short his holidays and flown back to deal with the emergency.

"To which Michael quipped:'Well manager, there's wan thing sure, you didn't sail here!'

"However at the height of the controversy over planning, where swathes of scenic countryside were being blighted by one-off housing, Michael's comparing of one heritage body to the Ku Klux Klan was an outlandish exaggeration and attracted a threat of legal action," Ms Lucey concluded.

— 10 —

Drink Driving and All That

In early 2013, many people were outraged when Kerry County Council passed the motion by Danny Healy-Rae calling for a relaxation of the drink driving laws for people in rural Ireland. The council agreed with the sentiment that people in more remote areas, especially, should be allowed drive after 'two to three' drinks.

But nobody should have been surprised. The Healy-Raes, after all, have been campaigning against what they see as over-stringent drink driving laws for decades. By now, the torch has been passed on to succeeding generations of the family. It should also be pointed out while the Healy-Raes have been in the pub trade for nearly a half-century, they are themselves very moderate drinkers, or non-drinkers. Danny, for instance, is a teetotaller.

Jackie Healy-Rae, who opened his bar in Kilgarvan in the late 1960's, never saw anything wrong with a person having a couple of drinks and driving away home afterwards at their ease. These people, he would say, never as much as took a briar off a ditch, were never in accidents and travelled quiet country roads which had very little motor traffic. As a Fianna Fáil county councillor in 1994, he not only vehemently opposed stricter drinking laws introduced by the then Fianna Fáil Environment Minister, Michael Smith, but also joined a national campaign to reject the laws. He was also critical of vintner organisations for not taking a proactive part in the campaign from the outset.

Smith was not for turning, however. As if to put a damper on the festive season, the new laws came into force on December 2, 1994. Gardaí started a crackdown on drink driving, publicans in some areas claimed trade was down by as much as 50 per cent and the whole thing was portrayed as yet another attack on rural Ireland. By 1995, a new rainbow coalition government was in office and some amendments were made to the laws. Crucially, however, there was no change to the controversial 80mg limit on a driver's level of alcohol. In 2011, the limit was later dropped to 50mgs and to 20mgs for learner and professional drivers in line with EU laws.

To the day he died, Jackie Healy-Rae believed the laws were too strict. Son Danny was being consistent with the family's line on the issue when he put his motion before Kerry County Council, in January 2013.

"The idea is to help those people in every parish who are isolated and who can't get out of their place at night. A lot of these people are living in

Jackie Healy-Rae pulling pints in his bar in Kilgarvan during an election campaign. (© macmonagle.com)

isolated rural areas where there's no public transport of any kind. They end up at home looking at the four walls, night in and night out, because they don't want to take the risk of losing their licence."

The motion was passed by five votes to three. Seven councillors abstained and twelve were absent when the vote was taken towards the end of a long meeting. All of those who voted in favour were involved in the pub trade in some way.

Danny Healy-Rae said the idea had originated from people who visited his clinics to discuss problems and issues and who had to leave immediately afterwards because they could not drink and drive home. 'Characters' were being isolated at home and falling into depression, or worse, he claimed.

He could see the merit in having a stricter law where there were massive traffic volumes and roads were busy. But, on the roads he was talking about, you couldn't do any more than 20 or 30 miles per hour. Having a few drinks was not a big deal and he couldn't see any issue with it. "I know there'll be opposition. I know that it will be (from) people in urban areas who have access to different outlets than the pub. But in rural parishes, that's all we have. All people want to do is talk to neighbours, talk to friends, play cards, talk about the match and the price of cattle, about such a lady going out with such a fella. It's harmless."

Notoriety on the media followed. There was barrage of publicity, not all of it favourable. An interview on *Today FM* radio with Ray D'Arcy was over in a couple of minutes when the presenter cut him off air without warning. D'Arcy said afterwards his blood began to boil when he heard Healy-Rae outlining his position on *Today FM* news. The councillor had said there was no safety issue because the proposal would only apply to minor roads.

D'Arcy agreed there should be an open discussion about loneliness in rural Ireland and there was a serious issue about rural isolation, but allowing people to drink and drive was not the answer, he argued.

Despite the widespread outcry against the drink driving permit proposal, there was some support for the proposal from other rural councillors. Cllr Michael Fahy, of Loughrea, Co Galway, was quoted as being 100 per cent behind the call. "We don't want to see people drunk, we're only talking about up to three pints," he said.

But, opposition was intense. Deputy Michael Healy-Rae, who also agreed with his brother's call, asked the Gardaí in Pearse Street, Dublin, to investigate death threats made against him, as a result. "Some of the emails are just beyond belief, simply awful, and the work of really nasty people," he said. "I've no problem with people disagreeing with me and am prepared to debate any issue with them, but some are hiding behind the social media and making outlandish statements."

The social media also went ape on the controversy. Danny Healy-Rae insisted he was heartened by support which was coming from as far away as Chile, in South America. "Some people in Chile could identify with what I was about. People living in remote hills and valleys in Chile have problems similar to ours."

An *Irish Examiner* poll of milk suppliers, linked with the ICMSA, showed a majority of farmers did not support the call. The survey found 56% disagreed or strongly disagreed with the Healy-Raes, although 43% broadly favoured some softening of drink-driving laws. Overall, just 18% strongly agreed rural drivers should be allowed drive after a few pints.

Commenting on the survey findings, Michael Healy-Rae said the figures did not surprise him. He noted 43% agreeing with the proposal was a very high figure. "Those figures wouldn't surprise me in the slightest. Naturally, some of the figures I would be talking about are for very rural, isolated areas with no public transport or other outlets for recreation, but that might not be the case for all farmers in other areas. In a general national sense, those figures would be accurate but, in parts of Kerry for example, 100% of people would agree with our proposal."

In May, a German TV crew was dispatched to Kilgarvan. The crew did its work in and around the Healy-Rae pub and an estimated two million Germans later tuned in to watch the publican councillor's debut on *Spiegel TV*, an investigative magazine programme that has been running since 1989. The segment was also available on the *Spiegel TV* website, which attracts an additional 100,000 hits per day.

A story by Majella O'Sullivan in the *Evening Herald*, on July 2, 2013, was headlined: "Achtung the eejit…millions of Germans laugh at Healy-Rae's pleas to ease drink driving laws."

Danny Healy-Rae behind the bar. (© macmonagle.com)

It showed images of the latest scenes of Ireland to hit television screens in Germany, adding that they hoped Angela Merkel, the powerful German politician who pulls EU purse strings, wasn't among the two million viewers.

Reporter O'Sullivan went on: "Drink-driving, a man described as a 'Guinness fan' and the political dynasty that is the Healy-Raes. About the only thing missing was Dustin the Turkey all over again.

Fresh from the assault on German ears that was Deutschland uber alles, *Spiegel TV* has aired a documentary on rural Ireland featuring Danny Healy-Rae's controversial battle to slacken drink-driving laws.

The Spiegel programme that takes a tongue in cheek look at the proposal ponders the question, 'Three Guinness is still okay, isn't it?' and looks at the politician who is "fighting for more merriness".

Filmed in Kilgarvan in May, the segment featured 'Francie', a 70-year-old pensioner on his high stool in Healy-Rae's pub. Francie, the narrator says, with his thick grey sideburns and green hat looks exactly as you would imagine a real Irishman to look.

"He has always driven to the pub…how else could he get home?" But gone are the days when you can drive home after a few pints, we are reminded, even in rural areas with no buses and taxis.

"A man must be allowed to drink a few pints. He has a right to it. And, by God, after two or three or four pints you should still be allowed on the road," says Francie.

According to Spiegel: "The voice of this folksy politician carries weight; Danny comes from an infamous political clan. His father Jackie was a member of parliament and irritated Irish city politicians like a poltergeist from the country for decades."

Programme producer Roman Lehberger insists his take on the issue isn't mocking but it presented with humour.

"The core of the story is a serious issue and one that resonates with a lot of Germans," he told the Herald.

On his impressions of Mr Healy-Rae, he added: "He's a good-natured guy who really looks out for his people.

"It's a little humorous the way it's presented but the subject matter for Danny Healy-Rae is a serious one."

There the *Herald's* take on the story ended. The negative nature of the controversy and the programme didn't seem to do Danny Healy-Rae, or brand Healy-Rae, any harm. In fact, the notoriety achieved may have helped business in Kilgarvan. Some German tourists have since been noticed around the village and the unmissable pub, taking a close-up look for themselves. They shoot photographs to show to friends back home.

The media storm also showed up huge differences in attitude between urban and rural Ireland – reflected on one hand by, largely, the Dublin-based media, and Healy-Rae thinking on the other. But, in the midst of all the commotion, the essential elements of what Danny Healy-Rae was at were all but missed.

The twin, core issues at play in the long saga are isolation and transport - not drink. The Healy-Raes have often been accused of generating their own publicity for political purposes, but Danny did not set out to do it on this occasion. Nobody was more surprised than he at all rumpus created by his motion.

It wasn't the first time demands were made for special provision in the law for rural drivers, he pointed out. The Healy-Raes were asking: Why all the fuss now? What's new? If anything, it's the media in all its modern forms that's gone way over the top, not us as a voice of rural Ireland, they were saying.

The Healy-Raes regularly claim many urban people just 'don't get us', or don't understand what it's like to live in a remote rural area. The person they talk for could be a stereotypical bachelor farmer, living alone and getting on in years, several miles from his nearest pub, which is often his only social outlet. He goes there for the company, enjoys a few drinks, and learns what's happening in the parish.

Many of these men are not heavy drinkers and could spend an hour, or more, over a pint. Their homes could be miles away down a long boreen and they might not meet another car on their journey. Neither are they the kind of people who are involved in headline-grabbing, fatal accidents, after consuming vast amounts of alcohol or other drugs.

But, these normally law-abiding people are now afraid to drive even after one drink, so they opt to stay at home. Small towns and villages don't have taxis, though some have hackneys. Public transport doesn't exist. As well as urban folk showing a lack of empathy with their country cousins on this issue, it is part of the deep-felt consensus that rural Ireland is being ruthlessly robbed of services.

Take the Healy-Raes' native Kilgarvan. The village once had six pubs; now it has three. Until recently, it had a police presence since the days of the RIC, in the 19th century, but its Garda station has now closed.

One thing is certain – there is some support in rural areas for Danny Healy-Rae's proposal, even if people are afraid to say so publicly. During the controversy, Jackie Healy-Rae, who had retired from politics at this stage, made an interesting observation. He congratulated the Gardaí who, he maintained, could be 'a lot tougher' on rural drivers. Depending on their attitude to drinking and driving, people could interpret that statement any way they liked.

A transport solution - that would also include people going to pubs - could help tackle isolation. Publicans, who have an obvious vested interest, have tried to get transport systems going in some areas, with limited success. A few publicans here and there regularly drive their customers home. Drinkers, of course, could also contribute to the cost of a dedicated pub transport service which, for practical reasons, would probably operate only at night.

The Healy-Raes have no chance of changing the drink driving laws, but at least the important issue of rural isolation is being highlighted. However, it could be argued, they and other elected representatives might achieve more, and get wider support, by concentrating on the essential isolation problem and on setting up decent transport systems for everyone in rural Ireland - not just drinkers.

11

The Grim Reaper Calls

Around the time the so-called plain people of Ireland were having their dinner on Friday, December 5, 2014, Jackie Healy-Rae died in Kerry General Hospital, Tralee, at the age of 83. He was surrounded by his family who had been maintaining a vigil at his bedside since his condition deteriorated earlier that week.

For some years, he had been troubled by one of his knees, for which he underwent surgery. He was unable to exercise, however, and other complications set in during the early months of 2014. He had been in Killarney Community Hospital and Kerry General Hospital a number of times in the last eight months of his life.

His legs could not support him, but he still left his sick bed to vote in the May local elections for Johnny, his grandson. Concerns grew in the last few weeks of his life and indications to the media from his family were that all was not well. In early November, he contracted suspected pneumonia and was treated in hospital intensive care and coronary care units.

On November 19, son Michael reported his father was 'fighting the mother of all battles' and his condition was said to be fair. He had been hospitalised since April and had spent only a few weeks at home in that time. His partner, Kathleen Cahill, could not believe how his condition worsened so quickly. "It wasn't like Jackie to go downhill that fast," she said later.

Family members were constantly back and over to Kerry General Hospital. When Kathleen visited him on December 2, he spoke of Christmas and she saw that as a sign he didn't think he was dying. But he did say to some of his children he had no hope and continued to weaken. As his life

Jackie's coffin being shouldered from the family premises.
(© macmonagle.com)

ebbed away, on December 5, the family gathered around him. A poignant vigil as they awaited the inevitable. He was unconscious and quietly departed at around 1.30pm, having earlier received the Last Rites.

As news of his passing spread, an emotional Johnny Healy-Rae described him as a larger than life character. "We're very lonesome for him at the moment. We all looked up to him. Nearly everything we're doing today, he started it in one way or another. He started it all himself and put it into place for us. He started with nothing and built himself up."

As he had lived, he remained the centre of media attention to the end. Word soon reached social media and radio stations. Within an hour or two, it was national news and the whole country knew by teatime. The six o'clock RTE television news carried a four-minute package by the station's southern editor, Paschal Sheehy, which again featured in the main nine o'clock news.

That evening, knots of Healy-Rae supporters gathered in one of his favourite haunts, the Failte Hotel, Killarney, owned by the O'Callaghan family, close friends. Many were in tears. This was the premises where he would host conclaves of cronies over a relaxing Canadian Club whiskey, or a Bailey's liqueur, on Saturday nights. Former Killarney town councillor Niall O'Callaghan, Independent, was one of the first to pay a public tribute: "People up the country didn't realise how good and how cute he was. He was very effective in the constituency."

The following day, December 6, the national newspapers gave his passing a spread. Across the top of its front page, the *Irish Examiner* headlined a story with the following quote from former Taoiseach Bertie Ahern: "He fought tooth and nail for the people he loved". Ahern said he was a great friend and very loyal.

Current Fianna Fáil leader Michael Martin said he had always been fond of Healy-Rae and admired his sheer determination to improve services for the people of Kerry. Fine Gael Minister for the Diaspora Jimmy Deenihan joined in, saying he was a long-standing, genuine friend who had been committed to the people he represented.

In the *Irish Independent*, political correspondent John Downing described him as a 'one-off maverick character' from a poor background who went on to amass considerable wealth, building the foundations of a family business empire which spanned plant hire, civil engineering, pubs and shops.

"Jackie Healy-Rae was an old school constituency advocate known for his folk wit and non-stop passionate declarations. To paraphrase himself, 'there was no way in the wide earthly world' he could refuse to promise a favour for a constituent," Downing wrote. "Urban snoots scoffed and his adversaries shook their heads in disbelief. But Healy-Rae was loved by thousands of Kerry South voters who backed him and his family in big numbers and also gloried in the entertainment value."

Also on Saturday, thousands of people began to flock to Kilgarvan, where he lay in repose in the newly-refurbished lounge area of the family pub. They came for about six hours. On Sunday, they started queuing 90 minutes before the appointed time of 4pm for filing past the remains. At one point, the queue stretched for about 400 metres along the street and up the winding Bog Road leading to his birthplace in Rae. People were standing three and four deep and a shuttle bus ferried mourners from the outskirts of the village.

"I suppose we should have expected this as he touched so many people throughout his life. He was involved in so many different things as well as politics - Irish music, farming, auctioneering for a short time and sport, of course," said Danny Healy-Rae, fighting back tears.

It had the trappings of a traditional wake and, even in death, Jackie Healy-Rae looked like a man on the campaign trail. They laid him out in his best suit and that essential tartan cap. An election sticker seeking a number one vote was on his left lapel. There, too, was a well-worn mobile phone. A baby bottle of Canadian Club, a prayer card with a photo of Pope Francis, copies of books published about him, and his hurley from the 1950s, during which he won Kerry county championships with his beloved Kilgarvan, were also in the coffin.

As mourners entered the premises, they observed a typical, larger-than-life picture of the politician displayed on a window sill. It showed him smiling broadly, his jacket slung over his shoulder like a man in election mode. Inside, women went around with large pots of tea and sandwiches were piled high on tables. Everyone agreed it was one of the biggest ever funeral gatherings in the county, with the attendance estimated at upwards of 10,000 over three days. Some people queued in the cold and rain for up to two hours.

Many stories about him were swopped and his humble beginnings on a small farm in the rugged foothills of Mangerton were also recalled. "My father used to say that he came down that road in a donkey and cart with his mother and if the worst happened, he could go back up there again," related Danny Healy-Rae.

Political figures present on Sunday included constituency rival and former Ceann Comhairle John O'Donoghue, former Tánaiste and Labour party leader Dick Spring, Cork Fianna Fáil TD Billy Kelleher, Fine Gael MEP Sean Kelly, former Kerry Fianna Fáil TD Thomas McEllistrim, former West Cork Fine Gael TD Paddy Sheehan, Independent Tipperary TD Mattie McGrath, former Fianna Fáil Cork TD Noel O'Flynn and Independent Kerry TD Tom Fleming.

Deputy Fleming said Jackie was underrated. "He had attributes above the normal. His feet were firmly on the ground and his strong point was his natural way of relating to people. And, of course, he had an enormous work rate - no holidays and no days off!"

Small farmer and supporter Jim Breen, from Sneem, Co Kerry, described him as a very normal, down-to-earth man and who was always approachable. "I think he was one of the best TDs ever to hit Dáil Éireann. There should be six or eight like him in every county."

Former taoisigh Brian Cowen and Bertie Ahern at the funeral.
(© macmonagle.com)

The coffin, topped by the red and white colours of Kilgarvan hurling club, was shouldered to the local church late that evening by family members. As if re-enacting an election rally from years before, they were evocatively flanked by men carrying pikes topped with blazing sods of turf. It was an eerily dramatic scene the man himself would have appreciated.

On Monday, December 8, people started to arrive in Kilgarvan from many parts of the country, about two and a half hours before the funeral Mass was due to begin. Men in flat caps bared their heads as they crossed themselves on entering the church; women spoke in low tones; friends of the politician shook hands and remained silent in keeping with the sombre mood of the occasion.

All was peaceful and some celebrity spotting was also going on. The locals wanted to know who was turning up. The air of calm was broken slightly as word went around that some political big-hitters were in town. St Patrick's Church was full to overflowing when former Fianna Fáil taoisigh Bertie Ahern and Brian Cowen strode into the churchyard with Senator Donie Cassidy. After some greetings from supporters, they stepped inside and took their places in the front pews. Other politicians, including Micheal Martin and former Cabinet minister and MEP Gerard Collins, came earlier and secured their seats.

Two, smartly-uniformed people sitting together in front of the altar caught the eye. Lieut Commander Patricia Butler represented President Michael D Higgins and Commandant Kieran Carey the Taoiseach, Enda Kenny.

Sporting figures included the renowned Kerry footballer of yesteryear, Mick O'Connell, from Valentia, who was once a member of Kerry County Council when Jackie was also a councillor. Another All-Ireland winning Kerry footballer, Mick Gleeson, a current member of the county council, was also there.

Musician Johnny Carroll, with whom Jackie Healy-Rae, on saxophone, once made a CD, was among the early arrivals, setting up his equipment about half way the down the church. The top trumpeter and his politician friend had also made a musical television appearance. Carroll recalled how a demand for bookings followed but Jackie was far too busy to go 'gigging', preferring instead the political stage. It was entirely apt that Carroll should play, touchingly, The Last Post and Nearer My God to Thee during the two-hour service.

Jackie was a man of eclectic musical tastes, especially jazz, traditional Irish and country. He counted Acker Bilk, Paddy Cole, Charley Pride, Johnny O'Leary and Jim Reeves among his favourite artistes, so it was only appropriate music should be an important part of the service. There was warm applause after his son Danny, on accordion, played traditional tunes with his daughters, Maura, Elaine, and Theresa. The main music for the Mass was, as might be expected, by a local group, the Healys, of Headford,

The congregation was composed chiefly of ordinary folk who had loyally voted for Jackie Healy-Rae for upwards of 40 years, 30 as a councillor and 14 as a TD. They had seen his career grow and bloom from that of county councillor to a household name on the national scene, leading to the establishment of a new and powerful political dynasty. There was a genuine feeling of sorrow as they sympathised with the grieving family, all in black and obviously moved.

It was, of course, firstly a family funeral. As the chief concelebrant of the Mass, Kilgarvan priest Fr Con Buckley, pointed out, Jackie was the patriarch and they had a suffered a great loss, describing him as a much-loved father, grandfather and family man.

The sadness of the occasion was leavened with a little humour here and there. In life, his mobile phones were always on the go and one of the gifts handed in was such a phone. Michael Healy-Rae reported afterwards that his phone was going throughout the Mass, with people looking for him. Fr Buckley asked people to ensure their phones were turned off, 'including you Danny', to laughter all round.

Just before Mass began, family members brought forward tokens to symbolise Jackie's life. Fr Kevin McNamara, an outgoing, voluble cleric not unlike the deceased in personality, explained how each item meant so much to his late friend. These included an accordion, a basket of turf, a hurley and a hurling jersey, an election canvassing card, the mobile phone, a toy JCB and that unmistakeable tartan cap, probably the most recognisable bit of headgear in all of Ireland.

The cortege making its way through Kilgarvan. (© macmonagle.com)

A lifetime in which the politician wore many caps was recounted; how he grew up the hard way carved by a rural background which gave him a close affinity with country people and their needs. Values he espoused all his life. That was the tenor of the homily delivered to mourners in pin-drop silence by Fr Buckley, who told how Jackie would ask permission to leave the local national school early to go home to foot turf which he would later sell in the village to help the family survive.

Mentioning the old aphorism that all politics is local, the village priest made a classical reference to Homer's Odyssey which arose from a 'local squabble' and said Jackie Healy-Rae's greatness was in never losing touch with his family roots and the people who elected him. All of which, the priest said, made him a true democrat.

"He was a unique man. Yet, in another sense, all his larger-than-life features were shaped by a youth in the grand rural culture of Kilgarvan. Even the scrabble for a living here in harder times was the school of life that moulded his indomitable character. A Healy from the Rae, or bog, his family were the Healy-Raes to distinguish them from other Healys in the locality. Sadly, the extent of his schooling was primary school in Kilgarvan.

People say that if he had schooling he'd have gone far, but maybe it would just have spoiled his rooted vision."

It was a long homily, but Fr Buckley held the attention of the congregation, recalling how Jackie had helped rear two families, his own and a step family, because of his father's disability. He compared the deceased politician with St Pope Paul II who also had endured hardship and hard work in his early life. "Jackie also learned in the real school of ordinary life and people and, like John Paul, they were the ones he always served".

But he also developed many other talents. "You might not think it seeing his rotund shape in later life, but he was a fine hurler, earning county championships with Kilgarvan," the priest went on. "They say he was the fastest thing on two feet to a ball over 10 to 15 yards; he was also noted as a cyclist and musician, founding a band and playing the melodeon and saxophone with distinction. He could do anything and even made a wheelchair for his father from old bicycle wheels."

Summing up, Fr Buckley, who was joined in the Mass by six other priests, said it was his courage, confidence, skill and homely touch which helped him get elected as a TD for the first time in 1997. He also brought a witty face to the hard world of politics and that's why he was loved, the priest opined. "Indeed, while he kept two governments in power, his concern always was to win concessions for his beloved south Kerry. For his focus was the people he loved rather than the remote party or EU agendas."

———————— • ————————

At the end of the Mass, Danny and Michael Healy-Rae both eulogised their father, at length, and received standing ovations. Danny, his voice trembling with emotion at times, said his father was a loyal, dedicated man in whom people confided and who did his 'level best' for them. When it was popular to criticise Bertie Ahern, as many in Fianna Fáil did, his father had stood up for Ahern, he declared.

Referring to deals his father had done with Ahern in return for supporting Fianna Fáil minority governments, Danny, who spoke for more than 30 minutes, said he had never made unreasonable requests and had only looked for what was achieveable. "He was offered a State car early on but told 'em he had his own car and that it wasn't for a State car he was elected. He only wanted to work for the people in his constituency."

As if reflecting his close bonds with his father, he said he just didn't know how life would go on, now that he had gone. "He has put me in a fine spot. It's him that should be here. I'd like to have gone before him. I'm so sorry he's gone. I'd rather go through the suffering he went through than to see him suffering."

Then it was the turn of Michael Healy-Rae, still wearing his cap, to address mourners. For a man who had battled all his life, it was fitting that his father's last fight was the toughest and, perhaps, the most heroic, he told them. "Right up to the end, he struggled to live. He did not give in, he never gave up. And it took an awful amount of time before his mighty heart finally gave out. We will always remember that he did not give up without fighting the mother of all battles."

The man who succeeded his father in the Dáil then turned on political opponents, some of whom were probably in the church. "To the people that have tried taking credit for his work I have only one message for you here today - please don't let yourselves down by trying to take credit for something that you never had a hand, act, or part in." On a humorous note, however, he invited the visiting politicians to stay around and see how money secured by his father had been spent in Kerry.

Michael said the family's only wish was that Jackie be remembered for helping people. Over the years, he had brought improvements to infrastructure and services all over Kerry and also prevented the closure of smaller hospitals in Cork and Kerry, he said.

"I don't think anyone would disagree with me when I say that my father put a massive effort into each and every day of his life," he went on before concluding with a deathbed message. "My father asked me to deliver one final message to the plain people of Ireland that he loved so well. What he asked me to say was thanks a thousand million for everything and don't worry, I'll be keeping a close eye on all of ye from above!"

Traffic backed up around Kilgarvan which came to a standstill as the coffin was shouldered from the church to the local cemetery, on the other

Cortege comes to a halt for Jackie's pony, Peg, outside the family bar.
(© macmonagle.com)

side of the village, in accordance with local tradition. Relays of the politician's supporters carried the coffin, draped in the tricolour and a Kilgarvan hurling jersey. Led by a Garda car and a JCB, symbolising his love of machinery, the cortege was followed by a large concourse of mourners on foot.

Being as much an event as a funeral, the occasion could not pass without some element of drama and stage management. The cortege suddenly came to a halt outside the family public house where it was joined by Jackie's pet pony, Peg, all sheen after a 'hairdo' and wash-down for the occasion. The animal, which had been waiting with her handler, Dick Harte, started neighing giddily when she saw the coffin. She moved towards the hearse and put her nose up against it. As they vied for a different type of picture, photographers gathered around the pony. "I'm convinced she knew he (Jackie) was in the coffin," Danny Healy-Rae said later.

Having bade her last farewell, Peg, still giddy, led the way on the final leg of the journey to the cemetery. All again in line with an old tradition in the family - that animals should be treated kindly and a belief that people who neglect animals never have any luck for it.

The last tribute of the day came from Jackie's grandson, Johnny Healy-Rae, a third generation politician and the youngest member of the dynasty. As if to mark the end of one era and the beginning of another, the youthful councillor was chosen to deliver a graveside oration. He had learned everything at the hands of the man they called 'Jackson', he said. "He instilled in us honesty and fair play. He was relentless in his work ethic and failure was not an option. Thank you from the bottom of my heart for all you have done for us. It is down to us to continue to fill his shoes and we will do that."

Chief mourners were his partner Kathleen Cahill; sons Danny, John, Denis, and Michael; daughters Joan and Rosemary; their mother, Julie; brothers Denny and Mick; sisters Hannie and Cathy; stepbrother Timmy and stepsister Peggy.

A man called Tommy Dunne, who had worked in forestry in Kilgarvan with Jackie in 1951/'52, travelled from Kildorrery, Co Cork, to the funeral. He also had stories to tell. Jackie had been working in forestry with a spade and Tommy was a bulldozer driver who taught him to drive the machine. At one stage, Tommy was away from the job for a few days, so Jackie then worked the machine. He related how, one day, an inspector visited the site and saw Jackie on the machine. Jackie thought he 'would get the road', but the inspector waved at him approvingly. After that, Jackie drove on - in every sense.

After the funeral, Tommy went into the bar and made himself known to the family. Danny remembered his father speaking about him and how he used to hurl with Kilgarvan. Tommy was the man that probably started Jackie in heavy machinery, leading to a successful plant hire enterprise, and they were glad to meet him.

What others said at the funeral

"He was a good guy to deal with, very honourable. He was only concerned about issues in his own constituency. He was hugely loyal and we knew he was never not going to support us (Fianna Fáil) because he was Fianna Fáil at heart. I never tried to woo him back to Fianna Fáil. In my own view, he would not have got elected had he run as a Fianna Fáil candidate in 1997, but he got massive publicity with his pictures all over the papers when he decided to stand as an independent."
– FORMER TAOISEACH BERTIE AHERN

"He was a character, one of the old characters, a throwback to a different time. He was able to adapt very well to modern politics and modern communications. He was a guy not to be underestimated. He was very knowledgeable about what his local priorities were and he was reasonable in his dealings. He knew when there was a bit of leverage to be used, but never overdid it."
– FORMER TAOISEACH BRIAN COWEN

"He was a very decent, courteous man whose use of language had the capacity to catch people's attention — his lyrical use of words. I remember getting a lovely letter from him about an embryonic Southdoc which he said was the most important letter I would ever read as minister for health."
– FIANNA FÁIL LEADER MICHEÁL MARTIN

"A most astute person, exceptionally intelligent, and someone who could communicate with people at all levels. He had an exceptional ability to attract media attention in a positive and entertaining way."
– FORMER FIANNA FÁIL MINISTER AND MEP GERARD COLLINS

"His character was a once-off and Kerry and the people of Kerry were his everlasting pride and joy and that was all that mattered to Jackie. I'm sure people in urban centres and Dublin, in particular, didn't understand that, but Jackie knew his people."
– TIPPERARY NORTH INDEPENDENT TD MICHAEL LOWRY

"Jackie proved he was a man of the people. He stood for the people of Kilgarvan and south Kerry and delivered for them and some national media poured scorn on him, but Jackie was a shrewd operator. He was able to negotiate and look after his people, but he had many national policies as well."
– TIPPERARY SOUTH INDEPENDENT TD MATTIE MCGRATH

"He was a great colleague on the council and lightened many serious debates with his sense of humour. I told him once that it would be only when he went independent that he'd go places. He has left an indelible mark in South Kerry."
– RENOWNED KERRY FOOTBALLER MICK O'CONNELL, AN INDEPENDENT MEMBER OF KERRY COUNTY COUNCIL WHEN JACKIE HEALY-RAE WAS A FIANNA FÁIL COUNCILLOR.

Death of Julie Healy-Rae

The passing of Julie Healy-Rae, on September 28, 2015, occasioned deep regret among her family and circle of friends. She died at her home in Scrahan Mews, Ross Road, Killarney, following a short illness. She was aged 84.

From Wilmington, Delaware, USA, she was raised in New York by her adoptive parents, Hannah (nee Healy), who hailed from Coolies, Muckross, Killarney, and Daniel Stephen Healy, a Kilgarvan native who fought in World War One with the US Forces. In 1953, she came on holidays to Kilgarvan where she met Jackie and they were married in St Patrick's Cathedral, New York, on August 6 that year. The couple lived in New York for a brief period before returning to Kilgarvan.

She worked in the Syrian consulate in the Empire State Building, could speak and write Arabic and was fluent in six, or seven, languages. She also studied psychology.

Remembered as an unassuming and gentle woman, her son Michael described her as a most special and intelligent person who would be greatly missed. "She believed that it was not the things that happen to you in life that are important, but how you react to them," he said.

Julie loved her pet dogs and was a keen card player, especially Bridge. Also well read, she liked to travel and was interested in politics and current affairs. She also embraced modern communications technology which helped keep her in better contact with her grandchildren.

Thousands of people paid her their last respects and extended condolences to her sons, Danny, John, Denis and Michael; daughters, Joan and Rosemary; grandchildren, great grandchildren, sons-in-law, daughters-in-law, brothers-in-law, nieces and nephews. She was predeceased by her sisters, Hannah Beale and Eileen Corrigan, who both lived in the US. Julie was laid to rest in Aghadoe Cemetery, Killarney, following Requiem Mass in St Mary's Cathedral, Killarney.

Speaking at the Mass, Michael Healy-Rae revealed it was his mother who encouraged her husband to adopt the Rae part of the surname. It was because of the townland he was born in and to distinguish him from all the other Healys, in Kilgarvan.

Julie Healy-Rae at her home with son Michael and her dog, Blondie.
(Naomi Gaffey, *VIP* magazine)

He told mourners in the packed cathedral it was fitting to celebrate the life of a great woman, who everybody remembered as a 'real lady'. He also revealed that when his mother arrived in Killarney, in 1953, she was met by a man named Michael Jones who introduced her to the taxi driver, John Healy, the man who later became Jackie Healy-Rae.

Julie passed away only nine months after her husband. They reared a family of six and, even though they had separated in 1977, they remained friends.

— 12 —

Danny Healy – Rae

On January 30, 1982, Danny and Eileen Healy-Rae got married. And they also had another important duty to perform. They attended a Fianna Fáil convention in Killarney, as delegates, that evening, to select candidates for a general election in February. The wedding celebrations went on. It's a story that tells a lot about Danny whose life has been dominated by politics and work from his early days.

As a child, he spent a deal of time on the farm at Rae with his paternal grandparents, Danny and Mary. He would push grandad's wheelchair around and do little jobs for grandmother, who was always busy. She was a smallish, but exceptionally strong woman 'with arms like Muhammed Ali' from hard work all her life, according to Danny. She had a strong voice, a big heart and loved singing.

Clearly, it was a kindly and welcoming house for a child. A kettle was always hissing on the crane over a turf fire and Mary kept the front door open all day long, Danny remembers fondly. If someone came into the yard, she would expect them to have tea and would be insulted if people didn't accept her hospitality. She was known as a woman that could cut turf as good as any man and would take the youngest child to the bog in a tea-chest.

Sometimes, Danny would sleep overnight in Rae and he can vividly recall the lights of his father's tractor shining into his bedroom. This was in the early 1960's and Jackie would be mowing hay for neighbouring farmers at night. In season, Jackie and his brother, Denny, would be out on hire round the clock, with Denny driving the tractor during the day.

While he has successful plant hire and pub businesses, it's the land that's

Danny with his grandfather, also Danny, at Rae. Grandad is in the wheelchair made for him by Jackie, many years before.

in Danny's blood. The farm at Rae has expanded greatly from the original 65 acres. Over the years, they purchased small adjoining farms, bringing the holding to around 200 acres, about 40 of which could be described as 'good'. The remainder is average, summer grazing land. They keep a suckler herd and no longer milk cows, but they cut turf there every year.

Danny looks every inch a farmer. A countryman's countryman. His open-neck shirt is as much a personal trademark as the tartan cap was to his father. He's constantly on the go and might visit four or five pubs on a single night on clinic business. His mobile phone is never turned off and is charged during normal sleeping hours. But he has received calls well into the small hours. For him, politics is a 24/7 occupation and part of his normal working life. He has an in-depth understanding of issues that affect rural people and farmers.

He and Eileen have a grown-up family of six: Johnny, Patie, Dan, Maura, Elaine and Teresa. He remembers his father as someone who never stopped working. Jackie always saw something to be done and would never put off until tomorrow what could be done today. At times, he wouldn't give himself time to sit down for a meal and would eat on the hoof.

Like his father, Danny has an easy, personal touch and is a good communicator. He's also blessed with a computer-like memory for first names, faces and even mobile phone numbers. He knows his Killarney Electoral Area, its people and their genealogy better than the back of his hand. Holidays are strangers to him. He and Eileen once went to Chicago for five days, but he felt an almost irresistible urge to fly back home after two days. "If you don't keep at it (work) and go away for a few days, there's a feeling that something might go wrong. I feel kinda guilty there's something to be done all the time."

A follower of football and hurling, he also loves traditional Irish music, also being a musician himself. Most years, he attends the All-Ireland Fleadh Cheoil for a few days, as well as the All-Ireland hurling final, and spends a night or two in Dublin whenever Kerry are in the football final.

He has also had a life-long interest in all sorts of machinery. At the age of 13, Danny was out mowing hay with clear instructions from his father, who 'knew every field in the parish'. He learnt much from his father, also a good ploughman and an excellent welder who could improvise with machinery if he didn't have the necessary parts handy.

Danny was involved in his father's political career since Jackie joined Kerry County Council, in 1973. He remembers local controversy in Kenmare when Jackie sought a nomination for co-option at the time. At the age of 18, or 19, Danny was also a Fianna Fáil delegate at local and constituency levels and travelled to political and other meetings with his father. He recalled going to the Rathmore area with him during the 1974 local elections campaign. When they were passing through the Bower area, the loudspeaker on their car was blaring out tunes from the Tulla Ceili Band. "The cows went mad – they were dancing in the fields," he recalled.

In 2003, he was co-opted to his father's county council seat. He was elected the following year and has retained the seat, polling impressively, since then. His brother, Michael, had been a councillor since 1999 and they sat side by side in the chamber until 2011 when Michael was elected to the Dáil. He and son Johnny now sit together on the council.

Danny also has the Healy-Rae penchant for attracting publicity. In October 2007, the little-known Kerry Slug crawled its way into the spotlight following a decision to re-route a small section of the proposed Macroom/Ballyvourney bypass, a major new roadway linking Cork and Kerry. Not for the first time, a member of a rare snail family stood in the way of road construction, like the snail on Pollardstown Fen, on the route of the Kildare bypass, previously.

Environmentalists explained the presence of such a creature highlighted the overall environmental value of the habitat. The Healy-Raes called for the slug to be transferred to some area well away from the route, but the expert advice was that couldn't be done. Hence, the need to conserve the habitat at the Cascade Wood site, near Ballyvourney. The EU can refuse to fund road building if such work threatens sensitive habitats.

First mooted almost 40 years ago, delays in building the bypass led to many complaints and some sceptical people believed the snail was used as a delaying tactic. However, the project was included in the Government's six-year, capital roads programme, announced in September 2015.

Believing that people should come before snails, Danny Healy-Rae has never accepted the snail case. "How did they know he was the Kerry Slug? Was he wearing a Kerry jersey?," he mused, wryly. "The snail is inside the ditch laughing at us trying to travel a road that two lorries can hardly pass on. There's no money available now for the road and the snails blocked it when the money was available."

In January 2013, he unexpectedly found himself at the centre of international media attention after Kerry County Council passed his motion calling for an easing of drink driving laws for people in rural areas. He agreed to take a phone call from Ray D'Arcy's *Today FM* radio programme, but the normally unflappable presenter hung up less than three minutes into the interview, dubbing the councillor's views as farcical.

"He was on the news before I went on air and I was just fuming just hearing him," said D'Arcy afterwards.

Danny and Jackie Healy-Rae. (© Valerie O'Sullivan)

Healy-Rae, however, has definitely has not changed his view on the hot issue. He said *Today FM* kept ringing all morning from about 7.30 onwards and kept him waiting until around 8.50 for the interview. All he wanted was a fair hearing and fair play which he always gave to people, but he did not get that, he argued. It was bad manners on D'Arcy's part to slam down the phone, he maintained, and the first time someone had hung up on him.

The presenter said whole thing was like something out of a Myles na gCopaleen novel and the programme had received several emails from Kerry people saying they were embarrassed by what was going on. "I hope it doesn't go global," he added. But global the story went.

Well before the referendum allowing same-sex marriage was passed, in May 2015, Danny Healy-Rae's views were known. He was one of a minority of Kerry county councillors who opposed a motion, more than two years earlier, by Labour Cllr Gillian Wharton-Slattery.

Her motion supporting same-sex marriage was passed by 18 votes to seven and the Kerry council became the 14th local authority to declare its support. The Healy-Raes, who normally back each other on issues, took opposing stands, with Johnny voting for the motion. Danny said he believed homosexual marriage was not 'natural' and he would have issues in relation to adoption, but stressed he had nothing against gay or lesbian people. He voted No in the referendum.

———————— • ————————

In December 2014, he turned his thoughts to wildlife and suggested birds may have more brains than some legislators. None of the feathered friends would be so silly as to build nests near a busy roadway, he maintained.

"To think that any bird would be foolish enough to build her nest where she'd be blown to pieces, and the feathers blown off her and she to be left standing naked in the middle of the road, never made sense to me. Birds have brains as well and they will build where it is safe to reproduce and feel safe," he declared at a county council meeting where criticism was voiced over hedge-cutting and burning restrictions under Wildlife Acts.

A perennial motion calling for a complete list of contractors employed by the council, and the amounts paid to each one, sometimes irks the Healy-Raes, who have been working as contractors for the council since Jackie started in the mid-1960's. According to information given to the March 2014 meeting, at the request of Independent Cllr Brendan Cronin, Healy-Rae Plant Hire Ltd, owned by Danny and Eileen, was the highest paid plant hire and haulage contractor to the council in the previous year. The firm received €294,192.

Danny Healy-Rae said the tendering process is not always understood and he proceeded to give a lengthy explanation. Anyone can put in a tender for a job, but certain requirements and the certification of drivers, for example, have to be satisfied. Other issues include price, service, tax compliance, quality of work and driver capability. "The money wasn't stolen. Everyone had to work hard for it, and the work and employees involved have to be of a certain standard," he stated, with fire and passion.

Planning has always been an area of huge interest to the Healy-Raes. They strongly believe people should be allowed build one-off houses on their own land in the countryside. They regularly call for an easing of what they see as over-restrictive planning. They have clashed many times with An Taisce and other organisations seeking greater protection for the environment, but are now finding themselves in increasing conflict with the National Roads Authority (NRA). Problem is the NRA is appealing to An Bord Pleanala against Kerry County Council decisions to grant planning for houses along national secondary roads, such as the Ring of Kerry and the Killarney to Mallow roads, which run through Healy-Rae heartland.

The NRA appeals, some of which have been allowed by Bord Pleanala, are usually on grounds of traffic hazards. The Healy-Raes generally do not agree with the NRA in these matters, pointing out the NRA is objecting to planning applications even when existing entrances to sites are being used.

Over the years, Danny Healy-Rae has become something of an expert in planning. He usually spends Sunday mornings calling to the homes of people who have planning problems and advises them. He believes strongly in visiting sites in order to get a first-hand grasp of what's involved, and then prepares a case to help an applicant.

During the economic boom, Kerry County Council zoned thousands of acres for housing and other development – six times more than was needed to meet demands. Councillors were being lobbied by landowners and developers, who were regularly seen at council meetings in those heady days.

In the wake of the recession, council management saw no need for all the zoned land and set about dezoning large chunks of it around the county. Danny disagreed, arguing that could leave all available zoned land in the hands of a small number of developers, who could then charge excessive prices. He feels the more zoned land the better, believing it would create more competition and bring down prices.

He also believes that, in future, developers should be given planning permission, initially, for only a phased amount of houses and that no further permissions should be given until a phased number had been completed.

One of his novel proposals, in 2015, was for a deer crossing, instead of a zebra crossing, for the village of Kilgarvan. Wild deer are now so numerous in villages around south Kerry that motorists have to be prepared to stop for them, just as they do for pedestrians, he told the council. Expert opinion,

Danny Healy-Rae and his wife, Eileen, pictured with their family at the wedding of son Johnny and Caroline. Standing are: Dan, Maura, Patie, Jackie Healy-Rae and his stepsister, Peggy, Theresa and Elaine.

he explained, is that once deer paths are established, they are stuck to rigidly and used by generations of deer, referencing a deer path at the edge of Kilgarvan village as an example. Motorists regularly have accidents with deer; he wants Killarney National Park to be fenced and all deer tagged.

Like other members of the family, he could attend several funerals in any given week. "I make no apology to anybody for attending funerals. It's a time-honoured tradition whereby you respect the dead and try to console people whose loved ones have died."

One of the reasons his mobile phone is never turned off is that he likes to respond rapidly to problems. Swift action and bypassing bureaucracy, in times of crisis, have been hallmarks of the Healy-Rae modus operandi for decades. His reaction to the flooding of houses in the Tullig area of Castleisland, in the early morning of January 24, 2014, after a night of torrential rain, is an example. Danny received a call from a resident shortly after 6am and immediately headed to Castleisland in his four-wheel drive jeep, arriving there some time after 7am. A little river had burst its banks, as floods poured down from higher ground.

Using sandbags, Danny worked with the Tullig residents and contacted both Kerry County Council and the Office of Public Works. The OPW got silt cleared from the river that day. Castleisland had not been in his electoral area prior to the last local elections, but he has established a strong foothold there, helping to grow the Healy-Rae support base in north Kerry.

———————————◦———————————

Michael Healy-Rae

Never far from the media glare, Michael Healy-Rae inhabits the often contradictory worlds of celebrity politician and so-called plain people. A regular on TV and radio chats shows, he's an accomplished media performer, well able to articulate his views and seems to revel in controversy.

In his early days in politics, he was often accused of trying to imitate his father, but he's undoubtedly very much his own man. He may not have the same charisma as Jackie, but he's a chip off the old block, planed and sanded. With a ready grasp of issues and scalpel-edge perception, he's also said to be better organised and more methodical in the way he goes about his political business.

Like his father, his main focus is on the constituency. All rural issues come within his bailiwick. Tackling rural crime is a priority and criminals targeting often elderly and vulnerable people in isolated areas should not be given the 'soft approach' any more, he believes. He also links the closure of rural Garda stations to the rise in burglaries and robberies.

The second member of the family to sit in Dáil Éireann is also a more modern politician and a user of the social media, with around 10,000 Facebook followers. Even before he first entered Kerry County Council, in 1999, rivals had noticed his astuteness and political nous. Like other members of the family, his apprenticeship began in childhood and he directed all three of his father's general election campaigns.

Born in 1967, he often accompanied his father to council meetings and was putting up election posters while still in short pants. The death of a TD, like that of any person, is a sad occasion. But for Michael Healy-Rae, as a child, it meant the thrill of time off from school and trips to different parts of the country. He would travel with his father to an often distant constituency for a by-election. He has special reason to remember the 1975 campaign that saw Maire Geoghegan-Quinn elected as a Fianna Fáil TD for Galway West, following the passing of her father. To this day, he shows a trace of a wound in his upper lip - the result of a fall from a pole and his first political battle scar.

To Michael Healy-Rae, politics is all about service. "What you are is a servant of the people and if you get any other ideas into your head, you're only a fool," he philosophised, bluntly. "We've expanded our support base by giving a sound, respectable and reliable service to the people. We want to do the right thing and the day we can't do the right thing we just won't do it anymore."

The Healy-Raes are seen as a political dynasty, but it's a term he dislikes. He prefers the description, 'family of politicians', saying that none of them own the seats they hold and are there are at the whim of the people. He sees nothing wrong with family members carrying on a tradition of politics. In fact, he believes it's an advantage for someone to have a family background in public life because they know exactly what's involved. Politics is about helping people, be it with local or national issues, as he sees it.

"Every person's problem, whether it's what you would call a small problem or a big problem, is their problem and it's the job of the politician to help them. You're a national politician because local people vote for you and then trust you. Remember, if you are fighting for nurses who are working in Kerry General Hospital, or in the community hospitals in Co Kerry, aren't you also in turn fighting for the nurses who are working in every hospital in the country? When I spoke about the closing of the Garda stations, wasn't that an issue that was affecting every community in the country!"

Like other members of the family, driving heavy machinery has always been part of his life. It was while bringing some machinery to Kilgarvan that he was involved in a serious accident, near Kilcoran Lodge, Co Tipperary, in 1990. His vehicle was hit from the rear by an articulated truck and he suffered serious leg injuries which left him on crutches for four and a half years. Following treatment and physiotherapy, he was back at work nine

Michael taking part in a celebrity charity cycle in Killarney, with an amused Jackie looking on. (© Valerie O'Sullivan)

months after the accident. One of the drivers employed by the Healy-Raes, Cathal O'Sullivan, would lift him body and bones over rough ground each morning and land him into the driver's seat of a digger.

In October 2007, he took park in a *Celebrities Go Wild* TV series with model Katy French and others in Connemara. He and Ms French struck up a friendship and he later attended her 24th birthday party in the Krystle Nightclub, Dublin, making her a present of one of his peaked caps. That was a happy occasion and he was shocked when Ms French died in tragic circumstances, in December 2007, four days after she had collapsed.

Michael Healy-Rae was the landslide winner of the *Celebrities Go Wild* series which resulted in the raising of thousands of euro for the People in Need charity. But the series had a controversial sequel, in 2011. People voted by phone for the contestants in the reality TV show. More than 3,600 votes for Healy-Rae came from within the Oireachtas and various government buildings. A phone bill of €2,639, was run up, according to the *Mail on Sunday* newspaper.

Both Michael, who was not a member of the Dáil, in 2007, and his father strongly denied making the calls. Jackie said he and his sons would have supported a number of people in their bid to become senators, so there would have been support for Michael from within Leinster House. TDs and senators are entitled to free phone calls by law, so no rules were broken in the case.

They can call local, national, mobile, premium rate and international numbers from their Leinster House offices. However, Taoiseach Enda Kenny and Ceann Comhairle Sean Barrett, pointing out the calls had not been made for Oireachtas business, called for the taxpayer to be reimbursed as there had been an 'outrageous' abuse of facilities.

While TDs' and senators' calls are not logged, it is the practice for phone service providers to inform the authorities when there are significant departures from normal call patterns coming from the main Leinster House number. But, the 2007 spike in calls was the only one noticed, according to the Oireachtas, in 2011. Though he paid the €2,639 bill, Michael Healy-Rae, denies to this day that he, or anyone belonging to him, had anything to do with the calls.

As phones had been taken from him, and other contestants, during their week in Connemara, he says he personally could not seek votes. He says he paid the bill because the controversy was affecting his work. "I must be the first man in Ireland to pay a phone bill belonging to other people."

In October 2013, he was reported to Gardaí after being filmed chatting on his hands-free phone and scribbling notes while driving, with a notebook resting on the steering wheel. He was one of several politicians who were filmed as part of an RTE documentary, *Looking After Number One*. Healy-Rae sparked a spate of complaints to the Road Safety Authority. Aware the cameras were on him in the car he was heard to say: "Oh God, you're not supposed to write and drive... there's some law about that."

He later apologised, but with a typical Healy-Rae rider that 'a person who never made a mistake never made anything' and said he never set out to deliberately do anything wrong.

Media fascination with the family reached a high point, in 2013, when hundreds of thousands of viewers watched a TV3 documentary, *At Home*

With The Healy-Raes. Reporter Ciara Doherty and a camera crew spent several days with the family when making the fly-on-the-wall programme in which Michael featured prominently. It showed the frenetic pace at which the family functions, day and night, and some revelations by Jackie on how he went about getting money from a cash-strapped Government, in 2010, for projects in the constituency.

An epidemic of rural crime and, as he sees it, the related issue of Garda station closures were brought home to Michael in a personal way, in 2014, when his home in Kilgarvan was broken into. The deputy, who was in America at the time, had previously warned the closure of Kilgarvan station would have disastrous consequences locally. A Kenmare-based patrol car was left to cover a large area of south Kerry and the Beara Peninsula, leaving people isolated and insecure.

The holder of certificates for three different guns, he urged people to apply for gun licences to protect themselves and their property. He believes firearms are very restricted in Ireland and linked to pest control and game hunting, or sports. A person has to be a member of a gun club, or own land, to be granted a licence. But, changes in rural Ireland mean communities now have to police themselves against ever-more aggressive and armed criminals. Whole swathes of the countryside are without a Garda station and the debate around legally held guns should be opened up, he believes. It may be time to extend the gun licensing categories for personal protection of home and property in rural Ireland, he maintains.

There are 220,000 firearms certificates on issue in the state, according to Gardaí, and these are renewed on a three-yearly basis. The vast majority of registered civilian firearms in Ireland are sporting shotguns and hunting rifles.

Language used by Healy-Rae to describe thieves preying on vulnerable people in rural area grows more robust. He has called them the 'lowest form of scum' and people that 'deserve to die roaring'. People are in a state of siege and living in fear, with doors bolted and gates padlocked, as he sees each day during his canvass in advance of the next general election.

While not advocating shooting thieves, he says homeowners are allowed to exert reasonable force when a burglar enters their property, adding that he wouldn't be sorry if a criminal went 'home in a box'. His message is people are not prepared to take the crime wave lying down any more. "The law says people can use reasonable force to defend themselves and their homes and it's up to people to determine what is reasonable force."

In April 2015, he again displayed a family facility for turning apparent criticism to political advantage. A leaked Fine Gael strategy document, prepared in advance of the next general election, included an assessment of candidates nationally. The document declared Healy-Rae to be 'unbeatable electorally', while also saying he 'hides behind the veneer of a friendly/simple country yokel'. He hit back, defending his rural roots and Kerry accent. "So, if you've a Kerry accent, Fine Gael are looking down their nose and they're laughing at you. People can like my accent, or lump it. I'll never try to be something I am not. If Fine Gael are insulting me, they're insulting an awful lot of Kerry people."

The document caused blushes in Fine Gael, which Healy-Rae exploited to the full. Jimmy Deenihan, Minister for the Diaspora and Kerry Fine Gael TD, denied any knowledge of it before the details became public. However, he agreed with the assessment Healy-Rae was 'unbeatable' in the next election – a view Healy-Rae would prefer not to hear, fearing it could give rise to complacency among potential voters.

Around the time of the document rumpus, ironically, Healy-Rae confirmed he had been approached by Fine Gael Finance Minister Michael Noonan and they discussed the possible support of four Independent TDs for a future, Fine Gael-led government. Healy-Rae, who has remained aloof from alliances of Independents in Leinster House, dismissed the move as premature. It can be taken, nevertheless, that his options will be open when it comes to the formation of the next government and he would never rule out entering agreements. He had previously been involved with his father in negotiating such agreements.

He claims there are only three 'true' Independents in the Dáil - himself, Michael Lowry, Tipperary North, and Noel Grealish, Galway West.

Conservative on social issues, Healy-Rae went against the national tide by voting No in the same-sex marriage referendum, in May 2015. Amid suggestions of ambivalence, some of his past opinions on the vexed issue were raked up. In a 2013 interview in the *RSVP* celebrity magazine, he said if two men, or two women, wanted to be together, let them do it. "Live and let live would be my attitude because life is very difficult," he was reported as saying then.

In the weeks preceding the referendum, however, he made his position clear. He did not see it as an equality issue; he was concerned about the way the liberal agenda was going; he had his reservations and would be untrue to himself if he voted Yes. But, he did not campaign for a No vote, believing people should be allowed make up their own minds. Even within his own, and the wider Healy-Rae family, people voted differently.

The Government; politicians and parties of all shades; celebrities like country music icon Daniel O'Donnell and Rose of Tralee Maria Walsh; sports heroes and people of influence all over the country were falling over each other in support of a Yes vote, which was carried nationally by a 62 per cent majority. So was Michael Healy-Rae out of step? In Kerry, 55 per cent of voters were in favour, but he was the only one of the county's six TDs to vote No, which meant he alone reflected the views of 45 per cent of county's electorate! At the referendum count, in Killarney, Fine Gael honchos took some glee from tallies that showed Kilgarvan had voted Yes by a slight majority.

The result was seen as a defeat for the Catholic Church, whose bishops had urged the faithful to vote No. Michael Healy-Rae is a Mass-going Catholic and his record shows he generally finds himself in agreement with the Church. He is totally opposed to abortion on-demand.

He's also opposed to the removal of Catholic and Christian symbols from public places and warmly welcomed RTE's decision to retain the 18 peals of the angelus bell, as a core part of Irish culture and community values. Plans to revamp the minute-long programme - broadcast on TV and radio Dáily at 12 noon and 6pm for over 60 years - were expected to remove the religious aspects and contain fewer Catholic elements. Healy-Rae praised RTE for its stance, stating any decision to remove the angelus bells from the programme would be disrespectful and not reflective of Irish public attitudes.

Regarding his faith, he tries to go to Mass at least once a week. "I find it

Michael and Eileen Healy-Rae and family. From left: Ian, Eileen, Rosie, Michael, Juliette and Jackie, with Kevin at front.

a great way to clear the head. I'm not a Holy Joe, but do I believe in God? Most definitely. And do I believe in Heaven and Hell? Most definitely."

Though portrayed as a strictly rural politician, he is also well able to represent people in urban areas and claims the 'two Ireland' concept – Dublin/Leinster versus The Rest - is driven and exaggerated by the media. Because of the negative and sometimes vile coverage the Healy-Raes receive in sections of the media, he is fighting back against what he describes as media bullying. He sometimes quotes lines from certain journalists like, 'I can no longer differentiate between the Healy-Rae pigs and the FF humans'. He has made it clear he will sue publications for defamation. A case by him against Independent News and Media was settled, with Kerry charities benefiting.

Some people in the media may be against the Healy-Raes because they don't conform like everybody else, he believes. Other observers, however, would say the Healy-Raes leave themselves open to caricature because of the way they present themselves and the sometimes colourful language they use – phraseology urban folk might find difficult to decipher. "Some of these journalists look down their big noses at us. That's it. I didn't go to university. Maybe if I'd gone to university they'd have more meas (respect) in me. I'd like to put to bed this parochial attitude people have about us nationally. They'd be happier if we didn't exist at all. And that is not right."

He's quick to react to constituency issues. In August 2015, when animal rights activists made their annual call to remove the goat from Puck Fair, in Killorglin, Michael Healy-Rae jumped to the defence of the age-old event with the alacrity of a mountain goat. Each year at the start of the three-day fair, a wild mountain goat is hoisted onto a 52ft platform in the town square, is crowned King Puck and presides over the shenanigans.

The Animal Rights Action Network claims the goat is treated cruelly and terrified while being kept in a small cage and exposed to noise and drunken revelry. Such claims were described by Healy-Rae as 'absolute nonsense'. He claimed the goat is well treated, fed and watered and returned to its mountain fastness in even better condition.

The goat, he told the nation, is under a vet's supervision; has its toenails cut, is checked for fluke and lice and savours an Egon Ronay-style diet of cabbage, hay and heather, with the leaves of an ash tree as a delicacy. The August fair, said to be over 400 years old, still has a strong primitive streak and a reputation as one of Ireland's great booze-ups, with pubs open until 3am each day. It has been said, with some justification, that everyone at Puck Fair acts the goat – except the goat himself!

With a huge work rate, Healy-Rae has managed to develop successful businesses and a political career at the same time. He and his wife, Eileen, have five children – Ian, Juliette, Rosie, Jackie and Kevin - all imbued with the family's work ethic. His declaration of interests under the Ethics in Public Office Act includes Roughty Plant Hire Ltd, based in Sandymount, Kilgarvan, while listed amongst his occupations are: postmaster, politician, farmer, and the owner of a filling station and a supermarket in Kilgarvan. He's also the owner of several properties.

Given his 24/7 political availability, he doesn't have much leisure time and holds clinics when many people are socialising. His clinic schedule could be the diary of a singer or a band. At 10 o'clock every Saturday night, he

Michael, Jackie and Danny Healy-Rae. (© Valerie O'Sullivan)

meets constituents in the Atlantic Bar, Kenmare, and every Sunday night between 10 and 11 o'clock in the family bar, in Kilgarvan. Farming takes his mind off politics and, like his father, he loves driving machinery. Shooting is another past-time, but opportunities for it are not as frequent. He also enjoys a late night walk to clear his head.

———————————◆———————————

— 14 —

Johnny Healy-Rae

Almost as soon as he was able to walk, Johnny Healy-Rae was 'tied' to his grandfather. As a toddler, he would accompany his grandad, whom they called Jackson, to Rae to milk the cows or travel further afield with him to fix breaks in public water mains with a JCB. Another place they went was the dump in Kenmare where they did weekly levelling work.

Before he ever set foot inside the door of national school, Johnny had been to annual meetings of Kerry County Council, where the chairman for the year ahead would be elected, and meetings of the Southern Health Board, in Cork. Jackie was, at different times, chairman of both bodies. From the top floor meeting chamber of Cork County Hall, Johnny would admire the sprawling city below and take note of Atkins farm machinery business where grandad would invariably stop to purchase parts for machines on their way home.

Much of their time together was spent on the farm at Rae. While grandad milked, Johnny would be filling buckets of ration for the cows. Often, the pressure was on during evening milking as Jackie might be heading to a meeting or have other political business to deal with. He would have something on every night.

After morning milking, Jackie would enter the family bar, put £5 in the till and take out the equivalent sum in 50p coins. He would then proceed to a public phone box in the pool room and start making calls to do with council affairs. Letters would also receive attention. Jackie could be heard on the phone, for some distance around, and, when he stopped talking, the lad knew it was time to go back to the farm. In 1993, Jackie got his first mobile phone which he later gave to Johnny.

Johnny with grandad Jackie, in 1997. (© Michelle Cooper-Galvin)

Johnny was blooded early in politics. He had his first election experience in 1991 – a local elections count at Aras Phadraig, Killarney. His father, Danny, brought the six-year-old along and they really had to 'squeeze tight' to get close to Jackie who was up beside a wooden cordon with his tallymen. Johnny has never forgotten the tension and excitement of the occasion.

But he had to wait until 1997 for his first active campaign - the year Jackie stood in a general election as an Independent candidate for the first time. Along with 20 or so other youngsters and a number of adults, Johnny would make up posters each evening. Jackie prioritised postering in his campaigns and it was always one of the matters he would check nightly.

Grandad was never slow to give Johnny responsibility as a child and, if he he didn't do something properly, he would be corrected. He came to know Jackie as an exact man in many ways and 'very tasty' with his hands. Jackie did all his own welding and repair work at Rae. He also cut all of his own silage, even after getting elected to the Dáil.

From his early days, Johnny came to admire him as someone who could always rise quickly from a setback and move on. There was a close general election count, in 2002, and people thought for a while that Jackie's seat was gone. The question was asked: what would he do if he lost? He put his hand on Johnny's shoulder and whispered: "I'll have to go back to the farm again. 'Tis (losing an election) something I can't do anything about."

In 2011, Michael Healy-Rae, after being elected in succession to his father as a TD, had to relinquish his seat on Kerry County Council. There was talk about who would succeed the new deputy on the council. One thing was certain - it was going to be a Healy-Rae. Johnny had a long conversation with grandad. Then 26, the young man was busy with the various family enterprises, including the farm and plant hire, and he wondered if he could give sufficient time to council business.

"It wasn't from a lack of interest in the council, as I'd always been interested in politics and there was plenty of political talk at home all the time, but I felt it might be difficult to manage everything," he recalled. "I also saw the commitment my father was giving to the council and felt it was nearly a full-time job if you wanted to do it right."

Michael and Danny also spoke to him and their view, shared by Jackie, was he should give it a try. Johnny was also 'getting itchy' himself and decided to have a go. His co-option to a seat for the Killorglin Electoral Area went ahead as planned, without opposition, on March 21, 2011. A father and son sat side-by-side in the chamber, ensuring the continuation of the dynasty into a third generation.

Proposed by his father, his co-option was seconded by Sinn Féin councillor Toireasa Ferris. The new councillor's mother, Eileen, Jackie and members of the extended family were in the crowded public gallery. As he had often attended meetings in the same chamber with his grandfather, he needed little introduction. Danny indicated the new member had the Healy-Rae work ethic and was following a tradition begun 38 years previously on the council.

Johnny now had three years to build up a profile and a work record in advance of the next local elections. He soon settled in. Sitting beside his father was a huge advantage, he acknowledged. Grandad, although now retired, would inquire regularly about what was going on and would advise him on putting down notices of motion. At meetings, father and son worked as a team, supporting each other and making robust contributions on issues such as planning, roads, housing, farming and rural problems.

During 2014 local elections campaign, Johnny traded on the family sales pitch, 'if a Healy-Rae can't get it for you, no one can', and also held forth on what he saw as the differences between the Healy-Raes and the political parties: "We're of the people. We work for the people. We have 80 clinics per month and deal with people on the ground. People are disillusioned with political parties and especially with the present government because of broken promises. They're also angry about water charges and property taxes which, in my view, are both unfair taxes because they don't take into account people's ability to pay."

Going before the people for the first time, the 29-year-old topped the poll in the redrawn South and West Kerry Electoral Area, securing an impressive 3,495 first preferences, 1,415 above the quota of 2,080.

Grandad was monitoring the results on Radio Kerry from his sick bed in Kerry General Hospital. "I hope he's proud of me because I was certainly proud of him when my uncle John collected him from hospital yesterday and he came to Kilgarvan to vote for me. I'd been tied to him from about the age of three and that's the honest truth," the newly-elected councillor told reporters.

He gave due credit to grandad's legacy, built up over 40 years, for his first election success. On the canvass, he had met people whom Jackie had dealt with through his work with machinery or farming – long before he was born!

Each night during the campaign, often quite late, Danny would visit Jackie in Kerry General Hospital and Johnny went over most nights. Johnny would joke that the first time he voted, it was for Jackie and grandad would now have to return the favour. In the course of a busy election campaign, Jackie did not want to see them hanging around the hospital for too long,

Johnny and Caroline Healy-Rae with their daughter, Maggie.

and told them so. The night before polling, Johnny told Jackie he did not have to come out to vote if he wasn't able. But the old man left the young man under no illusion – he was going to vote and no more about it.

The hospital staff felt it would be better if he didn't go, but he was insistent. Son John was given the job of collecting him and driving him to Kilgarvan to vote. As Jackie was unable to stand or walk, a polling clerk brought the ballot paper out to the car. Taking a ballot paper out of the polling station led to some controversy, but Johnny has since stated it was something that had previously been done in Kilgarvan for people with physical disabilities. Michael Healy-Rae was director of elections for both Danny and Johnny. The campaigns were conducted with typical precision and nothing was left to chance.

Johnny has been described as 'a pure Healy-Rae' and never goes anywhere without his notebook in the back pocket - hewn from the same rock as two previous generations of the family. He is married to Caroline (O'Mahony), a native of Templenoe, Kenmare, and they have a baby daughter, Maggie. Their wedding reception at the Gleneagle Hotel, Killarney, on December 29, 2012, broke all records. It was attended by 950 guests and the celebrations went on for three days.

The third generation Healy-Rae politician is the eldest of six children born to Danny and Eileen Healy-Rae. He owns the farm at Rae and also helps run the family plant hire business. Intelligent and astute, he comes across at times as being mature and politically battle-hardened beyond his years. A vocal councillor, he keeps his ear close to the ground. Unlike most people of his vintage, he doesn't have a Facebook page, nor does he tweet. Mobile phone and email are his main means of communication but, more than anything, he prefers face-to-face contact with people.

He's also a dedicated funeral-goer, explaining: "When a family loses someone, it's only a matter of courtesy to offer your sympathies. I never went to a funeral without knowing people. I go out of respect if I only knew the person who has died."

As a politician, his contributions are grounded. On a day, for example, when some fellow councillors were losing the run of themselves in relation to mountain wildfires, he highlighted the very pertinent issue of who would be responsible for compensating people whose homes, farm buildings or other property could be destroyed, as was quite likely, by these fires.

He believes wild deer are a major nuisance in the country and that herd sizes are out of control, citing damage to farmland and road accidents. He wants to get rid of the Japanese Sika deer and, in July 2014, claimed at a council meeting that deer are carriers of TB and therefore pose a serious threat to cattle.

"St Patrick got rid of the snakes and we're managing fine without them. It would be the same with the deer," he declared. "This is a bit like the Macroom bypass when there was more meas (respect) on a snail than on the people of Kerry. Things are now gone too far the other way. A farmer must fence in cattle and insure them. He is responsible if they go onto the public road. I want someone to be responsible for deer - the Department of Agriculture, the National Parks and Wildlife Service, or some state body. They (deer) have to be tracked and kept under control."

The Department of Agriculture initially rejected his claims that deer are responsible for the transmission of tuberculosis (TB) to cattle, but he later noted the department was no longer as sure in relation to deer spreading TB.

On a different issue, Johnny Healy-Rae was not satisfied with the way Kerry County Council went about getting land for a new greenway in south Kerry. Around €4m was allocated by the Government for a greenway on a disused railway line from Glenbeigh to Renard. It is being promoted as a money-spinning tourist attraction and one of the best things ever to happen the jobs-starved area.

Just over 100 landowners were involved and difficulties arose between the council and about ten of them. Johnny opposed the council's plan to proceed with compulsory acquisition (CPO) of land in all cases, claiming there would be no need for compulsory purchase if the council was more flexible in its approach. Some people's private houses and farm buildings were affected, but there were ways of getting around problems if, for example, the council was more prepared to deviate from the exact route of the old railway line, he felt.

For years, gorse-burning on mountainy land has caused difficulty for farmers and is a contentious issue. There's a ban on this type of burning between March 1 and August 31, but Johnny Healy-Rae wants the burning period extended widely, arguing that the farmer knows better than anyone the correct time to burn.

"It's all very well to have these time limits in countries where the climate is consistent and predictable," Johnny noted. "But, with our weather being so unpredictable, there should be more flexibility and it should be left to the discretion of the farmer. Farmers have also had their payments cut for not keeping their land free of gorse, so the farmer can't win."

Large-scale burning outside the permitted season causes serious damage in Kerry every year. Upwards of 4,500 acres were damaged in Killarney National Park by illegally-set fires, in 2015. Local lobbyists are urging Arts and Heritage Minister Heather Humphreys, who is reviewing the regulations, to introduce a system of planned gorse burning, with revised dates, as the only sensible way to control wild fires.

In February 2015, Healy-Rae came up with a proposal to have St Patrick's Day celebrations moved permanently to a Sunday to boost tourism. A precedent had already been set in some American and European cities which stage the celebrations on the weekend, or Sunday, nearest to March 17, he pointed out. But, he failed to get the backing of his council colleagues.

He got the idea from some restaurant owners Kenmare who felt that having St Patrick's Day on a midweek day was not of much use to anyone. People working away from home, who would like to be home for St Patrick's Day, would also appreciate the change and would be able to make a weekend of it. Having St Patrick's Day on a Sunday, he said, would mean the following day would be a bank holiday.

"I was disappointed and surprised at the reaction of other councillors because most people are very positive about my proposal," he said. "It would give a big lift to pubs, restaurants, hotels, and bed and breakfasts at a quiet time of the year. I intend to pursue it and will lobby the government as far as I can."

Johnny is also very much on-message with senior members of his clan in relation to allowing drivers in rural areas to take, maybe, two drinks before sitting behind the wheel and setting off home from the pub. He voted for Danny's proposal to that effect when it was passed by Kerry County Council.

People in cities and bigger towns did not understand what was behind the '100 percent valid motion', he argued. There are people living miles from anywhere whose lives are being seriously blighted by isolation and transport issues. He instanced the story of two pensioners living seven miles from the nearest bar and post office. Their home is reached by a long, winding country road and they don't have a mobile phone, a Facebook page or any modern communications gadgets.

"There's no hope they can get someone to drive them, or a taxi to bring them home. People living in Dublin, like Ray D'Arcy (radio presenter) don't understand what it's like to be these two people," he said. "They (D'Arcy and others) are far removed from the reality of the life they're talking about. I don't see anything wrong with the kind of people I'm talking about having a drink or two and driving up a road where they won't meet another car. People in cities and towns are high to the moon on drugs and there's no question about that, while innocent, decent country people are trapped in a life of isolation."

The Healy-Raes are either moderate drinkers, or teetotallers, and Johnny describes himself as an occasional drinker.

He voted Yes in the 2015 same-sex marriage referendum, taking a different line to his father and uncle. "It was a very difficult issue for a lot of people to make up their minds on. Coming from the younger generation, things change over time. I'd never want to impose a decision on anyone, whether right or wrong, if the only one it affects is themselves."

— 15 —

Three for the Price of One – How it Works

"We have our own party - the Healy-Rae party," Danny Healy-Rae jokingly boasted after the 2014 local elections. A more effective and better vote-hoovering machine than any of the established political parties, he might have added.

But, the Healy-Rae machine is not a political party as the term is understood; nor does it fit into the left, right or centre slots on the Irish political spectrum. The approach is populist and intensely local, based on service to the general public - giving the maximum number of people what they want and limiting restrictions, in planning for example, as far as possible. The approach is characterised by drive, focus and determination. There's no branch structure – this political machine is, rather, a network of trusted and tested key supporters in every corner of the constituency.

John O'Donoghue, of Farranfore, who cut his political teeth in Fianna Fáil, has the title of 'chairman' of the organisation in perpetuity. He's not exactly sure when the title was first conferred, but it happened prior to one of the early general elections in which Jackie was a candidate. It is Healy-Rae practice to convene a general meeting of 40 to 50 supporters at the start of an election campaign, with the Healy-Raes at the top table and O'Donoghue presiding. It was at one of those meetings Jackie received a surprise call on his mobile phone and reputedly asked the caller how they knew where he was!

In many ways, O'Donoghue is a good example of a key Healy-Rae supporter. His father, Tom, was an old IRA man, a friend of the late Fianna Fáil TD for Kerry North, Tom McEllistrim, and a devotee of the de Valera-founded party from its inception in 1926. As a youngster in the 1940's and '50s, he put up election posters for 'Tom Mac'. He was also involved in the 1966 by-election and has a clear memory of canvassing with high profile Fianna Fáil politicians such as ex-Dublin footballer Des Foley and Brian Lenihan. He remained active in the party until he followed Jackie Healy-Rae out of it in 1997.

"I thought Jackie was being wronged in not getting a nomination, which he deserved after all his time working for the party. He was a very popular man," O'Donoghue recalled. " A lot of us were also getting cheesed off as many older people in Fianna Fáil were giving the impression they resented the younger crowd."

O'Donoghue, a retired Kerry County Council clerk of works,

John O'Donoghue, Farranfore, pictured behind Michael Healy-Rae in the torch-lit rally which took place in Killarney prior to the 2007 general election.(© macmonagle.com)

didn't have much soul-searching to do before opting to become a disciple of Healy-Rae whom he first met, in 1967, when Healy-Rae was driving a digger on the site of the Scarteen Park housing estate, in Kenmare.

Prior to 1997, O'Donoghue had been a tallyman for Fianna Fáil at election counts and continued doing that necessary job for Healy-Rae. Like many others close to the Healy-Raes, he thinks there's no big secret behind their success as politicians. "They do the work and follow-up it up, which is most important," he summarised, quite simply. "They do their best for people and if they can't do something for people, they tell them."

The wheels under the Healy-Rae machine are stand-out supporters like O'Donoghue, in towns, villages and rural districts. Dedicated, willing people who are totally loyal to the Healy-Raes. Many have been there since Jackie started out and were once in Fianna Fáil. They can be relied on to tip off the family about local issues, funerals and other events, as well as giving the inside track on what's happening in a locality. They keep the family in touch with the grassroots and can arrange for people to contact the family. Some even make their homes available for clinics.

The Healy-Raes have managed to retain the support of a priceless corps of former Fianna Fáil people. Paudie O'Callaghan, of the Failte Hotel, Killarney, is close to the Healy-Raes. The Healy-Rae and O'Callaghan families have been friends for decades, a link stretching back to the days when they were all in Fianna Fáil. Paudie cites the mantra, 'hard work, work done', to crystalise the Healy-Rae political philosophy. "What makes them tick is that they're on the ground all the time. They're strangers to no one. They're not high-flyers around the place. They're down to earth and what you see is what you get," he said.

They attract people of different political outlooks and none. Jackie contested the 1997 election as Independent Fianna Fáil – a clever bit of political ear-tagging in that it made it easier for Fianna Fáil people to vote for him. But the family have long since dropped the party tag and are simply Independent, while retaining much of their former Fianna Fáil support.

Being independent offers the best of every world. As well as giving the freedom to take whatever stand they like on any number of issues, it also has many other advantages. The first is that, unlike other political dynasties which belong to a political party, the Healy-Rae machine is totally family-controlled. While dynastic families exercise a huge amount of control in their political parties, they are not always able to prevent the parties from putting forward other candidates who could be seen as rivals to the dynasty.

The biggest threat to a sitting TD is often within the party, with the situation in Fianna Fáil between Jackie Healy-Rae and the O'Learys, of Killarney, being a classic example. The Healy-Raes are fortunate in that they don't have that problem in their organisation. Here, you have a TD and two county councillors, all living in Kilgarvan: the councillors, being his brother and nephew, are most unlikely to undermine or oust the TD.

The three work as a team and if one man can't resolve a voter's problem, the expertise of the others is tapped into. This frequently happens.

As Danny Healy-Rae remarked:"Three heads are definitely better than one and there's always a way around a problem. One of us might have dealt with such and such a problem in the past - invaluable experience in cases like that. Experience is shared." The Healy-Raes admit to differences sometimes on issues, but if any serious differences ever arise they don't become public. The motto from The Three Musketeers is apt – one for all, all for one.

There are also mutual advantages for the Healy-Raes in having bottoms on seats in both Dáil Éireann and Kerry County Council. As a TD, Michael has two pairs of eyes and ears on the ground while he's away in Dublin. If he can't trust members of his own family, who can he trust?

Likewise, a councillor with a sibling, or close relative, in parliament is also perceived to have an advantage in that such a councillor has a direct link to someone at the centre of power, with access to state departments, civil servants and all that goes with that. Better still if the Independent TD is supporting the government of the day. The three Healy-Raes make the most of photo-opportunities when they appear in public together, as on the day of the opening of the Castleisland bypass. Again the message - three for the price of one.

In his book on Kerry's political dynasties, *Heirs To The Kingdom*, Owen O'Shea quoted politicians as agreeing that having a relative in national politics attracts voters to local authority candidates. While an ordinary county councillor might have to wait a long time before getting an answer from a department in Dublin, a councillor who is a TD's sibling could have a query processed through the TDs' enquiry system and get an answer almost immediately.

St Padre Pio was reputed to have the gift of bi-location. But brand Healy-Rae can do even better than that. Tri-location. The Healy-Raes rarely miss a funeral in the constituency. On days when there can be several funerals going on at the same time in scattered parts, a Healy Rae can be dispatched to each one. Funerals cannot be missed. "When you go into a house canvassing, people might say to you, 'the last time you were here, we had five (votes) for you – now we have only four'. If you weren't at the funeral you've no business going back there at election time looking for a vote," Jackie once pointed out.

There's a story, which may be apocryphal but could well be true, of an evening when there were three removals in three different areas of the constituency, some up to 40 miles apart. As Fianna Fáil had to be represented at all the removals, the party made a big effort to have three, prominent local politicians take a funeral each. Which was done. However, the story goes the three Healy-Raes – Jackie, Danny and Michael – turned up at all three.

Another advantage for a family of Independents working in unison is that there's a good chance the same people will vote for the brand in both general and local elections. In the 2014 local elections, for example, Danny and Johnny Healy-Rae topped the poll in their respective electoral areas, pulling in 8,000 first preference votes, almost two quotas, between them.

Michael Healy-Rae will be aiming to win a sizeable share of that brand Healy-Rae vote in the next general election. All that vote was picked up in the former Kerry South constituency, but Kerry is now one, five-seat constituency and Michael Healy-Rae will be going before voters in the northern half of Kerry for the first time. The votes secured by his brother and nephew would give him a handsome head-start as he heads into new territory.

While the Healy-Raes are rarely shy about taking credit for what they do for the constituency, their opponents sometimes accuse them of seeking credit for things done by other politicians. Rows about the Castleisland bypass and the new community hospital in Kenmare are examples of kudos being vigorously disputed. Former TD John O'Leary thought Jackie was lucky in 1997, but believes a lot of the projects and investment that came to south Kerry in subsequent years would have come anyway.

"The secret of the Healy-Rae machine is PR and the ability to say things and do things which get publicity. This idea of putting two posters on top of Carrauntoohill and having them photographed and published during the 2014 local elections was typical," O'Leary claimed in his memoir.

"As some photographer said to me one time, Jackie Healy-Rae would stand on his head if he knew the picture would appear somewhere. He could speak against something and then vote for it and he would keep talking as long as the press reporters were writing; he was a great man for political theatre. He had a great tendency to get people laughing when addressing a public meeting. For all that – and though it suits some to think otherwise – the Healy-Raes are very bright and whatever they turn their hand to, they're the hardest workers of the whole lot…Without doubt, after Neil Blaney, Jackie Healy-Rae was the best political operator I ever came across."

From time to time, the Healy-Raes come under the microscope because of their business interests, especially in relation to plant hire contracts with Kerry County Council. The family puts much of that down to plain, old-fashioned begrudgery and a lack of understanding of the tendering system for council work.

All three, current Healy-Rae politicians are also highly successful in business. In the Dáil register of members' interests, Michael lists his occupations as politician, postmaster, shopkeeper and plant hire company owner with local authority contracts. He also has more than 100 acres of land and several houses and apartments in different areas. Both Danny, who has the family pub, and Johnny are also in farming and plant hire, with council contracts.

Jackie himself drove a Mercedes, but they tend not to flaunt their prosperity and seem to live fairly ordinary, if hectic, lives. Hardly any time off, or holidays, though. Some Rae-watchers claim they don't give themselves time for leisure and enjoyment because of their near-obsessional devotion to work and politics. The Healy-Rae philosophy has always lauded a spirit of enterprise. They argue they have acquired what they have through their own initiative and hard work and make no apologies for that.

In April 2004, Danny faced a conflict of interest allegation on Kerry County Council. An investigation was carried out on foot of a motion by Independent Cllr Brendan Cronin who wanted to know if the then county manager, Martin Nolan, could guarantee a conflict of interest had not arisen in an issue.

The opinion of senior counsel Esmonde Keane was sought following a motion from which it emerged Danny Healy-Rae was the highest-earning, plant hire contractor with the council. His company earned over €400,000 the previous year from the council. He had attended a roads meeting in his own electoral area concerning the council's 2004 roadworks programme and had requested certain works be carried out, the county solicitor outlined to Mr Keane.

Mr Keane was asked whether a conflict of interest arose; whether Healy-Rae should have attended that meeting and whether he should be absent from the full council meeting in March where the roads programme for 2004 was to be finalised. The same thing seemed to arise in council sanitary services meetings because Healy-Rae might be selected to carry out digging and plant hire work in these too, the county solicitor wrote.

Plant hire work is not assigned at meetings, but by the council's machinery yard. It is the council area engineers who arrange roadworks and who, along with the machinery yard, choose contractors from the approved list, he also explained.

Mr Keane advised the council if a member was involved in finalising the list of approved contractors for roads, sanitary and housing, then he would be obliged to leave the meeting. Similarly, if any scheme to which a member, or a member's company, had been appointed as a contractor was to come before the council, any such member should declare his interest and withdraw. He should also absent himself where experience showed he had obtained a significant portion of work previously.

"In my view, however, in such circumstances in relation to, for example, the approval of the council's budget for the year, the interest of that member would be so remote or insignificant it was unlikely to carry weight," he said.

According to Mr Keane, a county councillor or member of a local authority is not required to absent himself from meetings on roads and sanitary services in which he has only a minor, beneficial interest. In particular, he should not have to leave meetings where the overall budget has been decided already and the only matters are the schemes to be proceeded with, even if he is on the list of approved contractors.

After counsel's opinion had been read, Danny Healy-Rae said he had been 100 per cent cleared of any aspersions cast against him. The questions arose out of a desire to hurt him politically, he claimed, and he had never taken part in discussions where a conflict of interest had arisen.

To some people, the Healy-Raes have come to symbolise much of what is wrong with politics in Ireland - the 'secret' deals which deliver favours to the constituency and the lengths to which they to go in pursuit of demands from voters. They have brought a style of politics, in which the client is central, to a fine art. As they see it, it's all about the constituency, serving the client and providing what has traditionally been expected of politicians in Ireland through an easily accessible clinic system.

The first commandment in Healy-Rae land is: thou shalt not turn off thy mobile phone. Never. One reason for such accessibility is that a problem can be dealt with promptly and, importantly from their point of view, before a rival gets to it. As well as reacting swiftly, they also try to get back to a client as soon as possible with an update on progress. They see themselves as champions of rural Ireland and rural issues. They continue to make hay from the consequences of a lack of any worthwhile regional policies, which has resulted in the ongoing decline of rural areas.

The number of people living in rural Ireland now makes up 38 per cent of the population, compared to 54 per cent five decades ago. People like Paddy Byrne, president of Muintir na Tire, constantly highlight these issues, pointing out the percentage in rural areas is dropping at a rate of 1 per cent every two to three years. Poor broadband services, the closure of schools and Garda stations, a rise in rural crime, emigration and the loss of services in villages and small towns all provide grist to the Healy-Rae mill.

Jackie Healy-Rae wouldn't have stood a chance of getting elected in Dublin. In many ways, the Healy-Raes personify the gap in outlook between city people and their country cousins. While some urban people, commentators and fellow politicians turn their guns on the Healy-Raes – not to mention the bile that regularly comes from anonymous warriors of the keyboard on social media – the family regularly receives poll-topping approval in Kerry.

Irish Times parliamentary correspondent Michael O'Regan believes the Healy-Raes have been victims of social snobbery, to a degree, and some unjustified ridicule at times. "But they've had the last laugh," he remarked.

Talk about gombeen politics and being lampooned in all sorts of media has never done them any harm with the Kerry electorate. The hackneyed Kerry joke, based on the shaky premise that people from the far south-west are stupid, is apposite. Once asked what he thought of Kerry's treatment in jokes, Hollywood star and Killarney man Michael Fassbender replied: "It's useful to play the part of a fool. Maybe that's what the Kerryman is about!" The Healy-Raes would understand.

The old belief that 'there's no such thing as bad publicity' seems to ring true. Far worse to be ignored by the media in all its forms. The *Waterford Whispers* website occasionally pokes gentle fun at the family, with the following, posted on May 18, 2015, being an example:

Undiscovered Tribe of Healy-Raes Found in Co. Kerry

"SKIN painted bright red, bald heads partially covered with peaked caps, arrows drawn back in the longbows and aimed square at a local search and rescue helicopter as it flew overhead. This is the first glimpse of a newly undiscovered tribe of Healy Raes taken in a remote part of county Kerry.

The contact took place near the Kerry border with West Cork after a routine search and rescue training mission was being carried out.

"We heard something hitting the belly of the chopper," wench-man Tommy Carey told Waterford Whispers News. "I looked down using the helicopter's CCTV camera and zoomed in, and to my surprise, I spotted five individuals in the woods below. They were firing at us as we passed over so we had to abort our training mission."

The apparent aggression shown by these people is quite understandable. For they are members of one of Earth's last uncontacted tribes of Healy Raes, who live in the remote region of the Macgillycuddy's Reeks, one of Ireland's highest mountain ranges.

Thought never to have had any contact with the outside world, experts examining the footage believe the tribe may have remained untouched for millennia and are thought to have their own form of democracy, similar to what we have in Ireland today.

"They seem to take care of their own people very well as the huts in their small village are quite big and extravagant," said Professor Gerry Thomas, a lecturer on indigenous tribes in the University of Limerick. "We also counted four, what we can only describe as pubs in the village, which is indicative of their tribe, considering there is only one hundred of them living there."

Kerry County Council has since forbidden contact with the village as it is usually a disaster for these remote tribespeople, who live a life probably unchanged for more than 10,000 years."

RTE southern editor Paschal Sheehy, who has known the Healy-Raes for decades going back to his days working for *The Kerryman*, believes the empathy Jackie had with people living outside cities and large towns and his natural likeability were critical to his appeal as a politician. "The expression about 'the people who have their dinner in the middle of the day' resonates with rural people and showed Healy-Rae's masterful use of phraseology and his ability to identify with the people who voted for him."

Many stories have been told about his gift of being able to read situations. There's an anecdote about a public meeting in Kenmare which Jackie attended, many years ago, and at which passionate views were expressed by both sides in a controversy. Having waited until the very end to speak, he told the meeting he 'agreed with every single word' said in the hall that night. He allowed everyone talk themselves out and both sides could draw the conclusion he was on their side.

The 'Raes' are not the natural successors to the great Kerry politician Daniel O'Connell, with his concern for slavery, Catholic Emancipation and his European outlook, who dominated national politics for three decades, according to Kerry journalist Anne Lucey. But, consciously or not, they have in significant ways borrowed the robes of the nephew of Hunting Cap.

"Caherciveen-born O'Connell conveyed his message with the aid of a carefully-crafted public image. Carriages, caps, torches, monster meetings were all employed," Ms Lucey says.

"Concerned about his baldness, O'Connell wore a wig. This was before he hit on his trademark cap. His green velvet and gold 'Milesian Cap' was worn in public and in private and a debate raged. The cap was considered a sign of O'Connell's buffoonery and backwardness, but was imitated by his followers. And while the debate raged, O'Connell, perhaps like the Healy-Raes, knew that while they were talking about the cap, they were also talking about the wearer!

"O'Connell was ridiculed in 19th century London for his cap: the almost bald Healy-Rae senior was ridiculed in sophisticated Dublin. Theatricality was part of the O'Connell machine, just as it is of the Healy-Rae's. The torch light parades, the tractor-led convoys at election time around the Ring of Kerry, the bar of a song on election, are all part of the Rae act.

"Be warned though, the Healy-Raes are not all fur cap and no brains. The media for the 'Raes' are the mass meetings of the 19th century: they know how to attract the cameras and the pens; they know how to organise a story, or put down a quirky motion, and with a large swathe of journalists they have close and friendly connections," Ms Lucey concludes.

Like O'Connell, images of Jackie Healy-Rae can be seen around Kerry, including veritable shrines in Killarney premises such as Scott's Hotel and the Fáilte Hotel. The bar in Scott's has a Jackie Healy-Rae Corner, featuring a glass case containing a tartan cap, a range of photographs and quotable quotes. There's a similar display in the Failte bar, across the street.

———————— • ————————

Epilogue

Recent American presidents, including Bill Clinton, were sometimes said to have been running a permanent campaign, as if they were always involved in an election campaign. Political scientists sometimes give a quite convoluted explanation of the 'permanent campaign' theory. But it could be applied to the Healy-Raes exactly as the words say. In their minds, once an election is over, the campaign for the next one begins.

They know most of a politician's work between elections is done far from view and the cacophony of the crowd. It's the phone calls, the emails, the text messages, the whispers in the ear, the clinics, letters that must be written, civil servants cajoled and arms that have to be twisted – all part of the daily workload. All that must happen before a politician – in Ireland at any rate - can bask in the glow of bright lights and be shouldered triumphantly from a count centre by supporters.

A Healy-Rae has never lost an election. Evidence of their political acumen over more than 40 years. While they can be as tough and as ruthless as anybody, they are friendly and work on a 'what you see is what you get' basis. No airs and graces. They're not trying to run with the Dublin 4 crowd; they hold their ground and don't apologise for what they stand for, with the drink driving controversy being an example of that. If people don't agree with them, so be it.

At a time when some rural folk speak in tones resonant of south county Dublin, or somewhere up in the air between this country and America, many people see the rich mosaic of accent and dialect in Ireland as under threat. But the Kerry accent is safe on Healy-Rae tongues. Pure country Kerry. To hell with those who mock us, they seem to say.

And there's that fundamental political savvy. Kerry journalist and former Fine Gael candidate Aidan O'Connor noted the Healy-Raes are excellent at sizing things up, very often taking what might be viewed as the populist stand. "They'd be great in a bookie's shop. They're Paddy Power material because they back the right horse, more often than not," he summed up.

The late Joe Walsh was a Fianna Fáil Agriculture Minister for the best part of a decade and achieved much as a politician. A TD for South West Cork, he was praised for his handling of the Foot and Mouth Disease crisis, in 2001; he delivered Common Agricultural Policy (CAP) reforms for Ireland in EU negotiations and had been chairman of EU Council of Agriculture Ministers. He also won several awards, including the Legion d'honneur, and served on a number of boards such as the Irish Horse Board. Yet, his death just a month before the passing of Jackie Healy-Rae received far less the coverage than that of the Kerryman.

RTE, for instance, gave a 30-second, voiceover report to Walsh's death, on November 9, 2014. In contrast, on the day Healy-Rae died, December 5, 2014, he received prominent coverage on RTE's six o'clock and nine o'clock television news – a four-minute slot each time comprising a pre-prepared obituary and a news reaction report by the station's southern editor, Paschal Sheehy. It ought to be pointed out, however, the funeral day coverage for both men on RTE was fairly equal.

Question: how did a politician of Joe Walsh's national and international stature, who achieved much for the country, warrant less coverage from the main national broadcaster, and the print media generally, than a politician concerned primarily with local issues in his constituency?

Students of politics could, no doubt, come up with various answers. One might be that the modern media is more interested in populist issues and the cult of celebrity rather than serious matters that might be seen as 'boring' to readers and listeners.

At the same time, the question might be answered in simply one word – personality. Healy-Rae brought the power of personality and colour to a new level in Irish politics. Many people listened to him, firstly, for entertainment and they also enjoyed watching him on television. He was a performer and a celebrity.

The *New York Times* once dubbed the mid-20th century Dublin Lord Mayor, Alfie Byrne, as a showman politician. The same description could well have been applied to Jackie Healy-Rae, albeit in a rural setting and a very different era. He never attended post-primary school; never took lessons in speech and drama, was never moulded by an education system which had scant regard for personalities that were different, and never saw a need to change his accent or to adapt his personality to suit others.

All of Jackie Healy-Rae's campaigns were personality-led. He might even have learned something from American, presidential-style campaigning, with music blaring from his election vehicles, noisy motorcades around the constituency, outsize posters with his photograph all over the place and torch-lit parades.

The Healy-Rae politicians are natural communicators and deft users of the media. Some high-profile politicians and business executives spend thousands of euro on communications and PR courses. The Healy-Raes are spared that expense, for they have natural ability to connect with people directly and through the media, as well as riding out controversies which don't tend to damage them in the eyes of the Kerry electorate.

And that's not to forget basic cop-on. A wise Kilgarvan neighbour noted, memorably: "You could be out of bed at six o'clock in the morning, but the Healy-Raes would still be up before you!" Figuratively and otherwise.

In Jackie Healy-Rae's own words

TO A CHEEKY FEMALE WHO ASKED IF HE TOOK OFF HIS CAP TO SCRATCH HIS HEAD
"Do you have to take off your knickers if you want to scratch your bottom?"

ON CHARLIE HAUGHEY
"I'd have to think twice before I'd die for any man, but if there was anyone worth dying for it was Charlie Haughey." (He revised his views later after the payment-to-politicians tribunal.)

ON NUDIST BEACHES
"If people want to go without clothes, why should they be made wear them? It's up to themselves in a secured beach in Ballybunion. We're not living in the grey old ages, for God almighty's sake."

ASKED IF BERTIE AHERN WOULD NOT DO A DEAL WITH HIM IN RETURN FOR HIS SUPPORT IN 1997, HE REPLIED:
"If that's the way he wants it, he can whistle his ducks to water." (Hump off in other words)

A THREAT TO PULL THE PLUG ON THE GOVERNMENT AND THEREBY FORCE AN ELECTION
"The fellas inside there (Dáil Éireann) can be buying oil for the chains of their bikes."

ON EX-FINE GAEL TAOISEACH GARRETT FITZGERALD WEARING TWO DIFFERENT SOCKS
"How can a man who can't put on his socks right in the morning be trusted to run the country?"

ON A RIVAL'S POORLY ATTENDED FINAL ELECTION RALLY
"You'd find more at the killing of a pig."

ON SUGGESTIONS DRINKERS SHOULD USE THE DART OR PUBLIC TRANSPORT TO GET HOME FROM THE PUB
"The only darts we've in Kilgarvan are the ones we've been firing at the walls for years."

A NON-SMOKER HIMSELF, HE OPPOSED THE BAN ON SMOKING IN PUBS
"This smoking ban is unworkable. Will the smoking police raid pubs and bring people up before the courts for enjoying a cigarette? If I still owned my pub and went up to some fella and told him that he'd have to go outside if he wanted a cigarette, I'd be sitting there by myself before much longer."

ON CONSTITUENCY RIVALRY WITH MINISTER JOHN O'DONOGHUE AFTER SIGNING AGREEMENT WITH TAOISEACH BERTIE AHERN, IN 1997
"Sure am I not propping him up and keeping him in his state car? I don't want to see him walking out of Killarney to Caherciveen without his car. Sure I'm the most valuable man he has. Am I not one of the three wheels under the Government?"

ON BEING SILENCED AT FIANNA FÁIL ARD FHEISEANNA
"You could be kept off the rostrum until a time when there wouldn't be television coverage or when the newspaper reporters and a lot of the crowd had left. Things could be manoeuvred that way and you'd find yourself talking to a near-empty hall. Nearly talking to yourself.

BISHOP EAMON CASEY WHO FLED TO THE US AFTER THE REVELATION THAT HE FATHERED A CHILD WITH AMERICAN DIVORCEE ANNIE MURPHY
"'Tis my honest view that Casey got a raw deal and what the man did was very light indeed compared with things that emerged about other churchmen afterwards. I think he should come back to Ireland and I'd love to welcome him."

A PUT DOWN TO A POLITICAL OPPONENT
"If you came into this world with only a shovel in your hand you'd die of starvation."

AFTER ALBERT REYNOLDS, FIANNA FÁIL, BECAME TAOISEACH, IN 1992
"I wouldn't cut, shovel or dig with him." (Healy-Rae was a high-profile Fianna Fáil councillor at the time).

ON THE MEDIA'S PREOCCUPATION WITH HIS HEALTH FOLLOWING A 'SCARE', IN 1998
"I'm perfect. I really had no health scare. If I sneezed here today, 'twould be all over the front pages of tomorrow's newspapers."

ON THE HAZARDS OF CANVASSING
"I had some fierce escapes from dogs, but I nearly bled to death after this cock drove his spurs through my shoe and cut my vein. I bate the bejabers out of him. He didn't attack the next time I called."

ON HARD-LUCK CASES
"Some people coming to me are so poor that they couldn't buy a jacket for a gooseberry."

ON FIRST BEING ELECTED AND REMAINING A TD
"The time had come for me to get in or get out and now that I'm in they'll find it damn hard to shift me."

HIS VIEW OF PADRAIG FLYNN FOLLOWING THE FORMER EU COMMISSIONER'S STATEMENTS ON THE LATE LATE SHOW ABOUT THE CHALLENGES HE FACED IN RUNNING THREE HOUSES
"I thought Flynn was an amazingly bright and powerful operator over in Brussels. But he walked into the soup the same as if he didn't have a clue what he was talking about. He really put his two feet in it. A major blunder altogether."

ON FIANNA FÁIL.
"One of the big regrets of my life is all the work I did to ensure the election of TDs for Fianna Fáil. It was the most thankless work of all and I often ended up with embarrassing jobs after elections. I was betrayed by the party."

ON DIFFICULTIES IN TRACKING HIM DOWN
"I'm on the road oftener than I'm at home."

AS HE BEGAN HIS CAMPAIGN AS AN INDEPENDENT CANDIDATE IN THE 1997 GENERAL ELECTION
"I'll be a good trespasser in Fianna Fáil territory."

AS THE SAME CAMPAIGN WENT ON, HE WAS GETTING A GOOD RESPONSE AT AFTER-MASS MEETINGS
"I wish to God there were two Sundays in the middle of the week."

ON A PROPOSAL BY JUSTICE MINISTER JOHN O'DONOGHUE, IN 2000, TO CLOSE DOWN PUBS FOR SERIOUS BREACHES OF THE LICENSING LAWS
"Jesus, man, that wouldn't be done in Russia."

TO AN INTERVIEWER CURIOUS ABOUT HIS HAIRSTYLE
"They're on about my auld hair all the time. I take no notice in the wide earthly world. One rub of the brush is all it takes. I don't give the day to it. I just try to make the best use of what I've left."

ON THE UBIQUITY OF THE HEALY-RAES
"We're everywhere   just like Santa Claus!"

THE POOR QUALITY OF HAY BEING EXPORTED DURING A BAD SUMMER, IN 1980
"You couldn't feed hens with it. 'Tis only fit for making birds' nests."

ON THE THEFT OF HIS PET PONY, PEG
"We'd every guard in Ireland after her. I'm not joking. The lads above (in Leinster House) were saying Peg is found and there's still no trace of Shergar!"

ON GETTING HOME TO KERRY
"I've just returned from Dublin. It's the only thing to do if you find yourself there."

DID HE EVER CONTEMPLATE DEFEAT IN AN ELECTION?
"If the people of south Kerry decide they don't want me any more, I'll go back to driving my JCB."

TO A FRIEND WHO ENQUIRED ABOUT HIS HEALTH A SHORT TIME BEFORE HE DIED
"I'm in the departure lounge - with a one-way ticket!"

Appendix

JACKIE HEALY-RAE
Kerry County Council, 1973 to 2003. Council chairman on two occasions. Also a member and chairman of the Southern Health Board. Member of Dáil Éireann, 1997-2011.

DANNY HEALY-RAE
Kerry County Council 2003 to 20-.

MICHAEL HEALY-RAE
Kerry County Council 1999 to 2011. Chairman on one occasion. Dáil Éireann: 2011 to 20-.

JOHNNY HEALY-RAE
Kerry County Council 2011 to 20-.

Bibliography

BOOKS

The Years of the Great Test 1926-'39, Thomas Davis Lectures, edited by Francis MacManus (Mercier Press 1967)

In A Quiet Land, John O'Donoghue (Batsford 1957)

The Course of Irish History, edited by T.W. Moody and F.X. Martin (Mercier 1984)

Rule 42 And All That, Sean Kelly (Gill & Macmillan 2007)

The Mighty Healy-Rae, Donal Hickey (Marino Books 1997)

On The Doorsteps, memoirs of a long-serving TD, John O'Leary (Irish Political Memoirs 2015)

Heirs To The Kingdom, Owen O'Shea, (The O'Brien Press 2011)

Irish Life & Lore, Kerry Collection Seventh Series (Maurice and Jane O'Keeffe 2014)

NEWSPAPERS & MAGAZINES

The Cork Examiner
Evening Echo
Irish Examiner
FarmExam
The Farmer's Journal
News Of The World
Sunday World
The Irish Press
Irish Independent
Evening Herald
Boston Globe
New York Times
Sunday Independent
Sunday Tribune
The Irish Times
The Kerryman
The Corkman

Kerry's Eye
The Kingdom
Now And Then
Killarney Advertiser
Killarney Outlook
South Kerry Advertiser
The Sunday Business Post
The Irish Mail On Sunday
Ireland On Sunday
The Clare Champion
The Sun
The Irish Dáily Star
The Irish Dáily Mirror
Hot Press
RSVP magazine
VIP magazine
Kerry GAA Yearbook 1982

WEBSITES

www.oireachtas.ie
www.electionsireland.org
www.thejournal.ie
www.killarneytoday.com

www.jackiehealyrae.com
www.kildarestreet.com
www.waterfordwhispersnews.com

RADIO & TELEVISION

Radio Kerry
Kerry Today
RTE
Today With Sean O'Rourke
Today FM
Newstalk
The Week In Politics

Prime Time
Cloch Le Carn
Morning Ireland
TG4
TV3
RTE Raidio na Gaeltachta
Spiegel TV, Germany

Index

Index